OLLY
MURS

OLLY MURS

MURS

The Biography

Justin Lewis

JOHN BLAKE

Published by John Blake Publishing Ltd,
3 Bramber Court, 2 Bramber Road,
London W14 9PB, England

www.johnblakepublishing.co.uk

www.facebook.com/Johnblakepub   facebook

twitter.com/johnblakepub   twitter

First published in paperback in 2012

ISBN: 978 1 85782 953 2

British Library Cataloguing-in-Publication Data:

A catalogue record for this book is available from the British Library.

Design by www.envydesign.co.uk

Printed and bound in Great Britain by CPI Group (UK) Ltd

1 3 5 7 9 10 8 6 4 2

Papers used by John Blake Publishing are natural, recyclable products made
from wood grown in sustainable forests. The manufacturing processes conform
to the environmental regulations of the country of origin.

Every attempt has been made to contact the relevant copyright-holders,
but some were unobtainable. We would be grateful if the
appropriate people could contact us.

CONTENTS

INTRODUCTION   vii

CHAPTER ONE BOY WONDER   1

CHAPTER TWO BACKGROUND SINGER   11

CHAPTER THREE DAY JOBS   21

CHAPTER FOUR TAKING THE RISK   33

CHAPTER FIVE THE ENTERTAINER   43

CHAPTER SIX SURVIVING THE SING-OFF   53

CHAPTER SEVEN BACK STORIES   65

CHAPTER EIGHT THE HOMECOMING   75

CHAPTER NINE A NATIONAL OBSESSION   85

CHAPTER TEN FINAL AND AFTERMATH   95

CHAPTER ELEVEN SYCOVILLE   107

CHAPTER TWELVE HEY MR SONGWRITER   115

CHAPTER THIRTEEN LETTING GO   125

CHAPTER FOURTEEN STAR QUALITY   137

CHAPTER FIFTEEN WHATEVER NEXT?   147

CHAPTER SIXTEEN IN CASE   157
  YOU DIDN'T KNOW

CHAPTER SEVENTEEN XTRA TIME   169

CHAPTER EIGHTEEN UNLUCKY IN LOVE? 179

CHAPTER NINETEEN ESSEX BOY   193

CHAPTER TWENTY OLLY AND   201
  CHARITY WORK

CHAPTER TWENTY-ONE PLANET MURS   211

CHAPTER TWENTY-TWO THE LIFE   223
  OF A SINGER

OLLY MURS UK DISCOGRAPHY   227

INTRODUCTION

Who could have predicted that, since finishing as the 2009 runner-up on ITV1's *The X Factor*, Essex boy Olly Murs would have flourished as one of British pop's recent success stories? Yet that is just what has happened. The handsome performer with the tight trousers and soulful voice has enjoyed a string of hits – 'Please Don't Let Me Go', 'Thinking of Me', 'Heart Skips A Beat' and 'Dance With Me Tonight' – most of which he has co-written. He has recorded platinum-selling albums and sold out numerous live venues. He has become a TV presenter and participated in numerous charity events. He has sung with Robbie Williams, and even with the Muppets. And last, but by no means least, he has become a pin-up and scream idol.

It all seems a far cry from his life before his *X Factor* experience. He had been a semi-professional footballer for the non-league club in his native Essex town of Witham but had worked in offices during the week. He had been just an ordinary guy in his twenties who would clown around, singing and dancing for his colleagues and family. Before long, he would get the chance to do the same for millions. He would audition for Simon Cowell and co. on *The X Factor*. He would become a star in Britain. By the summer of 2012, he was preparing to launch himself in America as the opening act on One Direction's live tour.

In this book, we'll see how Olly Murs – the cheeky chappie with the tight trousers and trilbies – became such a big star in such a relatively short time. We will find out just how hard he works, and where his motivation and drive come from.

Olly Murs is not just a singer and dancer. He's an *entertainer*. This is his story.

CHAPTER ONE

BOY WONDER

On Thursday, 25 June 2009, an audience gathered at the Excel Centre in London's Docklands area to watch the last of four days of auditions for probably the most popular entertainment show on British television. Since its inception in 2004, *The X Factor*, created by Simon Cowell, had been a weekend fixture on ITV1 in the autumn months leading up to Christmas. It aimed to showcase and then celebrate new singing talent on peak-time television. Millions tuned in every weekend to watch. And when each series was over, many would buy the finalists' recordings and tickets for their live concerts.

For this sixth series of *The X Factor*, though, to be screened from August 2009, a new twist had been added to the audition process. In previous runs, hopeful candidates would sing and dance in front of the judges in a small room. It would be seen by millions of viewers later but, in the heat of the moment, cruelty or encouragement would be delivered in this intimate environment. All this would change for series six. As with Simon Cowell's other cash cow for ITV, *Britain's Got Talent*, hopefuls would face a live audience as well as the judging panel. For the very first time, this live audience would have some input into the atmosphere of the tense initial audition process – although the judges' decisions would still be final. The crowd might be shrieking with approval but, if the panel gave four 'no's', that was that and the hopeful was gone.

At audition stage, acts would compete for inclusion in four categories: Girls, Boys, Groups and Over-25s. The latter category could attract the most surprising and unexpected people. The pop scene seemed to prioritise youth but it was never too late to push yourself forward to try your luck in an audition. Take for instance 48-year-old Susan Boyle who, just months earlier in April 2009, had become a TV and internet sensation on a global scale after she sang 'I Dreamed a Dream' on *Britain's Got Talent* to an astonished studio audience and judging panel. And on this June afternoon, after approving a rendition of Frank Sinatra's 'Come Fly with Me' by an 82-year-old former dance teacher (who insisted, 'This is my last chance'), the panel of Louis Walsh, Dannii Minogue, Cheryl Cole and Simon Cowell would witness a 25-year-old with seemingly limitless energy and charisma.

Simon Cowell later recalled that when Olly Murs took the stage that Thursday afternoon, he was immediately struck by his self-assuredness and by how relaxed he seemed in front of 2,500 spectators. 'There was nothing pretentious about him. He wore his heart on his sleeve. I felt the audience related to him as well.'

'I didn't think too much about what was going on around me,' Olly said later. 'I just did my job and tried to forget that it was so big.'

Before he sang, Olly was asked what his dream was. His answer was simple, ambitious and direct: 'To be a pop star and be famous, and sell records, and be an international superstar.' He then took his opportunity to impress panel and audience with a song 12 years older than he was.

'Superstition' was written and first performed by the singer, songwriter, producer and multi-instrumentalist Stevie Wonder in 1972. As with other performers Murs idolised, like Michael Jackson and Justin Timberlake, Wonder had established himself as a superstar by his teenage years. He was just 13 when his breakthrough hit, 'Fingertips', had topped the US charts in 1963, and by his 25th birthday had created a series of ingenious and groundbreaking pop, soul and funk LPs like *Innervisions* and *Talking Book*.

Watched back again now, Olly's performance of 'Superstition' is not technically perfect by any means. From time to time, his vocal falters and lags behind the beat of the backing track. But there is no question that, from the opening bars, he is communicating with both the judges and the audience, even sneaking in a faux-moonwalk as a nod to one of his idols, Michael Jackson (whose untimely death, spookily, would be announced within hours).

As Olly finished to a chorus of cheers, whoops and screams, he called out, 'Hey, come on!' He was already collectively engaged with the crowd, even though there were far too many faces to engage with on an individual basis. And joining in with the applause was the legendarily hard-to-please Simon Cowell.

Simon Cowell told Olly that he had made it to Stage 3 of the competition – what was known as 'bootcamp' – with the words 'the easiest "yes" I've ever given', adding, 'You are very, very, very cool.'

The other three panellists were pleased too. Dannii Minogue assured Olly that he had the 'whole package'. Cheryl Cole pronounced him 'a natural-born entertainer'. 'You've got four yes's,' announced Louis Walsh. Perhaps a lot more than four, reckoned Dannii: 'Everyone in the room. Two thousand yes's.'

With the sound of the crowd still ringing in his ears, Olly Murs left the stage to the strains of another Stevie Wonder hit, 'For Once in My Life' – a fitting choice of song. You may only get one chance to prove yourself as a potential star. Olly took that chance and it was the start of an extraordinary rise to fame.

Olly had attempted the *X Factor* audition process twice before, in fact, but reasoned, 'I felt I had to keep trying.' He had sung to backroom researchers and production-team members on his two previous attempts but knew that, to tickle the ear of Simon Cowell, 'You need to pick the right song.' Third time around, with 'Superstition', he picked right.

'It's a weird feeling when you first walk out on *The X Factor*,' Olly would tell ITV1 in 2012. 'The nerves, of course, because you know you've got to perform. The excitement because you're on one of the biggest TV shows in the country. And then you've still got the four judges in front of you.'

A collision of television and the music industry, *The X Factor* was not just about entertainment, it was about cold, hard business sense. Contestants who succeeded on the programme, even those who compelled the audience to watch and vote week after week, were not guaranteed to persuade the public to buy or download a track they would release six months after the series final. 'People can give an amazing performance on the show but then they can't get the whole career thing right,' argued Simon Cowell. 'It's disappointing but it's out of our hands – it comes down to the public – whether or not they like them after the show.'

The gifted winner of the 2006 series, singer Leona Lewis, had become a hard act to follow. She had sold millions of records, and not just in Britain. For Cowell, her international reach was the key to the sort of talent he wanted to foster from the base of the British *X Factor*. 'I want to find someone who is going to represent this country all over the world. And when you hear their record on the radio, you want to say, "This show helped to launch your career." One minute you're singing in your bedroom, suddenly you can be a star all over the world. Winning this show can change someone's life forever.' For Simon Cowell, it really was that simple.

Yet there was no guarantee of finding a Leona Lewis every time. There were the fates of Steve Brookstein (the first-series victor in 2004) and the 2007 winner, Leon Jackson, to consider. Once the excitement of the competition was over, success on the artistes' own terms was far from certain. 'We can't guarantee that they will be an international star,' Cowell would say. 'There is a fifty-fifty chance that they are going to make it. Sometimes it doesn't work. Trying to find a star with long-term appeal is not an easy job.' In late 2009, nine months after Alexandra Burke had stormed the 2008 final and landed the Christmas number one, it was still too early to say whether her career would go the way of Lewis's or of Brookstein's. 'This is not a career card, this is a platform,' Cheryl Cole pointed out. 'It's after the show that you actually prove yourself as an artist and the career kicks in.'

The press wondered if 2009 might be the year that a male artist with staying power could win both the series and establish themselves with a long-lasting pop career. The *Sun* newspaper lumped together a few potential finalists, including singing teacher Danyl Johnson and Jamie 'Afro' Archer (who sported a 'bubble-barnet' and described Essex's Olly Murs as 'the karaoke equivalent of telly chef Jamie Oliver'). When a large number of newcomers appear on television, the media has to use broad strokes to sum them up – where they hail from, what well-loved star they may recall, etc. No one really knows for sure who is going to be a superstar. Not even the British television-watching public. Not even Simon Cowell.

ITV1 broadcast Olly Murs's audition as part of *The X Factor* on Saturday, 12 September 2009. An estimated 12 million viewers tuned in to see him take the stage to the strains of Dennis Waterman's 'I Could Be So Good for You', the theme to the old ITV drama series *Minder*. He was presented as the epitome of an ordinary 20-something guy, whom many viewers could identify with. Until relatively recently, his experience of singing had been confined to posing in front of the bedroom mirror and joining in songs at family gatherings. Some pub-goers in his Essex hometown had seen him in action on karaoke nights and in a band or two but, outside Witham, almost no one in the music industry or the British public knew who he was.

But even at this early stage, Olly had self-confidence in spades. Within a few days of his singing debut on TV, he would say, 'I don't want to sound big-headed or anything but I've got something special – I'm not just someone who can sing. I can dance and sing.' He also suspected that his dancing ability gave him an edge over the previous winners of the contest, especially the males. 'Leon Jackson, Shayne Ward [who won *X Factor* in 2005], Steve Brookstein are all good singers,' he stressed. 'Maybe better than me. But I've got the dancing and I know that will put me ahead.'

To even consider taking a step into the limelight requires a great deal of self-belief and self-confidence. Those who are doubtful about their abilities could be swayed by the nay-sayers and pierced by critical slings and arrows. Pop stardom is not a suitable career choice for the shrinking violet or for those who hate being photographed. Olly recognised in himself that he was a shy person. 'But that doesn't stop me from knowing I've got talent,' he said.

The phrase 'overnight sensation' is much overused in entertainment circles. Even if someone becomes known to the general public with suddenness, it may be that they are known to entertainment-industry insiders. After all, millions of pounds are spent on launching a new artist – a big risk even for someone who is prodigiously talented and versatile. Uncovering an unknown – a *complete* unknown – can have many pitfalls. Yet, aside from some gigs in his hometown, Olly Murs did seem to be someone with genuinely untapped potential. And now, 12-million people had seen him on national television.

The Internet was similarly buzzing about Olly Murs. Some 350,000 visitors to the YouTube website would watch his debut appearance. Several Olly fan pages would be set up on the social-networking site Facebook, whose US-born founder, Mark Zuckerberg, was coincidentally born on the exact same day as him. It seemed everyone wanted to be Olly's friend. 'It's gone crazy, I've never been so popular,' he gasped. 'All these girls are messaging me and saying I'm hot. It's a shock because I've never been the guy that pulled all the girls. I haven't had a proper girlfriend for years.'

Olly Murs was, by pop's standards, a late starter. It's comparatively rare for a pop-music singer to emerge apparently fully formed in their mid-twenties and maintain their popularity after a year or two. But his *X Factor* debut was little short of sensational. Here was a performer who, in his formative years, had watched and heard the most accomplished dancers and singers, and assimilated all their greatest qualities, but had remembered to add something of his own too. 'My little shimmy from the audition is my signature.' But, he added, 'My dance moves never got me anywhere before.'

Even his parents were startled by his capabilities on stage. Pete and Vicky-Lynn had seen him perform in local bars a few times but the live audition was a different proposition. As we will see, they had expressed doubts about the job security of their son making a living as a singer and had tried to convince Olly that he should keep pursuing some kind of 'normal' employment. But all their reservations were swept away when they heard him perform 'Superstition' in front of thousands – and in front of the most critical voice in TV and music entertainment. 'They are like any parents,' said Olly. 'They want me to have a good job and a career, and didn't think singing was a long-term option. I think I changed their minds.'

But it's one thing to perform for family and friends. They're already rooting for you before you've sung a note. 'I love performing and all my mates have seen me dance in the clubs in Chelmsford. Now, not just my mates have seen me.' Olly Murs's emergence seemed sudden, but it had been a long time in coming.

CHAPTER TWO

BACKGROUND
SINGER

Long before Olly Murs' birth, and even before Simon Cowell's in 1959, the popular talent show was a mainstay of the TV schedules. Within months of ITV's launch in 1955 as commercial opposition to the BBC, the avuncular Hughie Green was presiding over *Opportunity Knocks*, in which variety acts new to television (some prodigious, others eccentric) were given a three-minute shop window to entertain the public on national TV. After a contraption called a 'clapometer' measured the applause of the studio audience for each act, viewers at home were invited to vote by post for which one they would like to see return on the next show. In this way, acts like the comedian Les Dawson, singer Mary Hopkin and comic poet Pam Ayres made a breakthrough.

Running for 22 years until 1978, *Opportunity Knocks* was essentially a kindly show, letting the audience make the decision over its favourites. But from 1973, it was joined in the schedules by the Saturday-night series *New Faces*, unearthing fresh faces like comic songwriter Victoria Wood and teenage impressionist Lenny Henry. Its most successful musical discovery was the eight-piece rock'n'roll group from Leicester, Showaddywaddy, who racked up many hits between 1974 and the early 1980s.

What *New Faces* inaugurated was a star panel of judges who passed comment on the acts. Though many of the guest pundits (entertainers, DJs, comedians) encouraged these rising stars, the ones who grabbed the headlines were two record producers and songwriters. Tony Hatch had made a name as a composer of TV theme tunes – some, like *Emmerdale* (formerly *Emmerdale Farm*) and the Australian serial *Neighbours*, survive to this day – and had written and produced pop hits like Petula Clark's international smash hit of the mid-1960s, 'Downtown'. Producer Mickie Most's formidable list of credits during the 1960s and 1970s included hits for Lulu, The Animals, Donovan, Herman's Hermits and Suzi Quatro.

Hatch and Most could praise acts, too, but they are remembered for being blunt, outspoken and direct if they felt an act wasn't up to scratch. Some thought them cruel but they acted as a balance to the often supportive comments elsewhere on the panel, and had a perspective from behind the scenes that the performer judges did not necessarily share. And one viewer watching at home who greatly enjoyed Hatch and Most's contributions to the show (who indeed loved talent shows in general) was the teenage son of an EMI record executive. 'I remember thinking those two were hilarious,' Simon Cowell told ITV's *The Talent Show Story* in 2012.

Cowell loved the speciality acts (spectacular, risky or just downright odd) which sometimes turned up on *Opportunity Knocks* and *New Faces*. He could see that they were the natural successors to circus performers. And Olly Murs was part of an extended family that stretched way back to the Big Top. His great-grandparents Edward and Kathe Murs, who hailed from Latvia in north-eastern Europe, toured the world as circus acrobats in the 1920s and 1930s. In 2009, their daughter-in-law Maureen recalled some of their crowd-pleasing antics: 'My husband's mother used to balance a pole carrying Edward on her mouth while he stood on top playing a guitar and performing other tricks.' Three years after the end of the Second World War, in 1948, Edward and Kathe settled in England.

Maureen's own son, Pete, was born in the same year as Simon Cowell: 1959. In the early 1980s, some 20 years before Matt Lucas and David Walliams would dream up the character of Vicky Pollard for television's *Little Britain*, Pete married someone actually called Vicky-Lynn Pollard, who was born in 1961. Their first child, daughter Fay, arrived in October 1982 and was soon followed, on 14 May 1984, by twin sons. They were named Oliver and Ben. Olly was born 15 minutes before Ben.

Olly's childhood was an idyllic one, with a great deal of love and support. 'I was lucky to have a great upbringing and lots of love. You're just so carefree, you just don't care what's happening.' The only wobble in his well-being as a youngster came when he had to have grommets (tiny tubes) inserted into his ear because he could not hear properly. Fortunately, his hearing would be fine thereafter.

Pete Murs, whose trade was toolmaking, was always music-mad. The family home was forever filled with the sounds of his eclectic record collection. Music even became the soundtrack to household chores, usually hastily completed just before Vicky-Lynn arrived home. 'My dad used to do the cleaning round the house,' remembered Olly many years later. 'And he'd put T. Rex on, and the Hoover would come out, the ironing board. "Right, Mum's home in a couple of hours, get this done!"'

'He was such a good boy at school, a little angel,' was Vicky-Lynn's memory of Olly as a child, also describing him as 'a mummy's boy who was never naughty'. For his part, he enjoyed his education and claimed never to have skipped classes. 'I always had one hundred per cent attendance because I loved being at school.' Though his reasons for attending may have not just been academic. 'I was always hanging around with the girls, trying to be Mr Smooth.'

'It's not shocked me, what he's doing now,' Pete would say after Olly became a national star, 'because he's always sung at home. You'd be shouting upstairs to him, "Dinner's ready!" You'd open the door, he'd be posing and dancing.'

The influence of music was assimilated by all three

Murs children, to the delight and amusement of the grown-ups. Visits to their nan's house would be enlivened by impromptu performances of the much-loved Proclaimers hit of 1988, 'I'm Gonna Be (500 Miles)'. 'Me and my twin brother Ben, and my sister, were all around the same sort of age,' Olly told BBC Radio 2's Ken Bruce in April 2012. 'She used to love us entertaining her 'cause we were just scatty, cheeky kids. And for us to be good, she used to get us to sing this song! 'Cause it made her laugh. We never knew the words – we just used to make it up as you go along.' For their reinterpretation of the Scottish twins' greatest hit, the three children were rewarded with the prize of chocolate biscuits.

Celebratory family gatherings often had a musical element. 'My nan's side of the family used to do a lot of singing,' said Olly. 'My auntie Pat used to be a singer in the West End and stuff like that, so there's always been some musical side to the family. So we used to have dancing, a lot of parties.' This was the early days of karaoke, singing to backing tracks, and the Murs clan were fast in acquiring a karaoke machine. 'It was almost like "Pass the Mic". The mic used to go round the room and everyone used to sing a song.' Olly has particularly fond memories of one of his solo spots at a New Year's Eve party that made everyone in the room burst out laughing – the cheesy 1992 country hit 'Achy Breaky Heart' by Billy Ray Cyrus, dad of Miley Cyrus.

Although both *Opportunity Knocks* and *New Faces* enjoyed brief revivals on TV in the years after Olly Murs's birth, the big TV talent-show phenomenon during his boyhood and teens was *Stars in Their Eyes*, which began on ITV in 1990. Hosted over a 15-year period, originally by Leslie Crowther, then by Matthew Kelly and, finally, by Cat Deeley, its premise was simple and unchanging. In an age where households like the Murs lapped up karaoke contests (a pastime which had spread across the globe from its origin in Japan), the series gave the ordinary viewer the chance to dress up and sing as their musical idol. They would walk through the doors, surrounded by dry ice, and emerge in costume as anyone from Shirley Bassey to Chris de Burgh. Part talent contest, part fancy-dress party, the series did not really discover new stars, at least none who would become long-term artists in their own right because they were aping their idols (though often extremely well).

In the same vein, the 1990s brought the outbreak of the 'tribute band', most notably The Bootleg Beatles and Abba revivalists Björn Again, where famous but inactive groups were recreated as authentically as possible for live performance. But, as with *Stars in Their Eyes*, the appeal of cover versions had its limitations in terms of spawning credible recording artists. Though there were always revivals of old songs in the charts, what made pop music novel and exciting was a sense of newness. The industry needed people who had personality and charisma, and their *own* personality and charisma at that.

Every Sunday evening, the Murs family would gather excitedly round the radio, listening to the newly unveiled

Top 40 singles chart. 'Sunday nights was like my equivalent of a Friday night now,' said Olly. 'I used to love Sunday nights, even though I used to go to school the next day and I used to dread it.' Michael Jackson, who was ever-present in the charts in the 1980s and 1990s, was a special favourite of all the kids.

Yet the charts of the 1990s had very few solo pop idols, at least in Britain. The Britpop boom in the middle of the decade was all about groups, not soloists – Blur, Pulp, Oasis, Supergrass, etc. And in mainstream pop that appealed to the very young, the vocal group held sway, especially boy bands from both sides of the Atlantic – New Kids on the Block, Take That, Boyzone, N*Sync, the Backstreet Boys, Five and, eventually, in 1999, Westlife. Add to that a couple of girl-group sensations in The Spice Girls and All Saints and it seemed like there were no solo singers around for Olly Murs to identify with. The only emerging solo superstar seemed to be Robbie Williams and even he had come from boy band Take That.

Not that that stopped Olly from loving Five and the Backstreet Boys or, for that matter, The Spice Girls. He had also idolised Justin Timberlake and Michael Jackson, before visits to festivals in his early adulthood started to broaden his tastes. 'I used to like a lot of pop bands, like boy bands, and Coldplay were the first band that I got into that made me a bit more credible. Coldplay sort of opened up to me the indie kind of vibe while still being poppy.' From that stepping stone, Olly started to delve into his dad's capacious, wide-ranging record collection, finding particular pleasure in the likes of 1970s icons like David Bowie and T. Rex's Marc Bolan, or British ska of the early 1980s like Madness and The Specials. It was a turning point. Olly did not turn his back on pop but began to embrace other types of music too.

In 2000, when ITV bought the format of a show called *Popstars* (which had been popular in Australia and New Zealand), its aim was to form and launch a new group on the British pop scene, with the help of a panel. Some of the panel would be nice, others not so nice. Simon Cowell, heavily involved in launching Westlife (managed by Louis Walsh), was asked to take part as the panel's Mr. Nasty. He said no, and a producer and former choreographer called Nigel Lythgoe took his place. Imagine Cowell's horror when the series turned out to be the TV hit of early 2001. The finished group, a quintet called Hear'Say, raced to number one, selling half a million copies of their debut single in just one week. In the group's ranks were Kym Marsh (now of *Coronation Street*) and the future TV presenter Myleene Klass.

Within a year, Cowell was persuaded to join the show when the format was rejigged to launch a solo star. But what really annoyed him about his involvement in *Pop Idol*, apart from Will Young beating his favoured protégé Gareth Gates to the title, was that he did not own the series format. 'My competitors had the recording rights,' he said, 'and it was actually making me feel sick.' It was this frustration which led to him approaching ITV with a new idea in early 2004. He craved more creative control and, with *The X Factor*, he got that. He also made sure that the judging panel had to do something themselves and so a panel of mentors was introduced.

The X Factor would bring together many facets from the talent shows of old. The viewing public would have the final say, but not before a panel of judges (some 'nice', some 'nasty') could sound off. Eliminating contestants each week was a feature shared with the reality-TV sensation *Big Brother*. Like *Stars in Their Eyes*, it would showcase talented singers covering familiar songs but here, these existed to see if a singer was infusing the song with enough of their own identity, to see if they would be able to make it after the series was over, with specially written and unknown material. Lastly, like *Popstars* and *Pop Idol*, but unlike the talent shows of old, *The X Factor* would televise the backstage audition process, in which both the prodigious and the sadly hopeless would be seen valiantly battling it out for the judges' attention. This feature of the show, so often criticised as exploitative and cruel for placing the spotlight on the deluded and even vulnerable, would nevertheless be enormously popular with the viewing public. Even a bad act could be compulsive viewing for 30 seconds – if only because it caught people's attention, unable to believe what they were watching.

Ultimately, though, the point of *The X Factor* (like all its predecessors) was to find a talent *and* a long-term star. Cowell did not want to uncover an able musical performer who then preferred to stay in the background songwriting (as had happened with David Sneddon, who had won the BBC's talent search, *Fame Academy*, in 2002). Cowell wanted someone who yearned for the fame and who was prepared to work hard for that exposure, *and* who could convey a charismatic personality which could charm the viewing public. It was hard to know why someone might have the 'X Factor' – that mystery ingredient – but he remained determined to hunt it down.

The first five series of *The X Factor* found great talent in its winning acts, notably in Leona Lewis and Alexandra Burke, both performers with exceptional vocal prowess. But by the sixth series in 2009, it became clear that someone was needed who might not have the most flawless vocal talent but could engage with the audience nonetheless. Could Simon Cowell have finally found someone in that vein? Enter Oliver Stanley Murs.

CHAPTER THREE

DAY JOBS

Though Olly Murs loved singing and dancing at an early age, he never thought of performing as his destiny. 'I was always in the background. It was my brother who used to do all the singing and dancing.' Sister Fay agreed that he was something of a dark horse. 'He was a very different Olly to the one you see on TV. He wasn't always the centre of attention and was certainly the quieter one.' But while he did occasionally perform in public to a wider audience, notably in a Howbridge Junior School production of *Joseph and the Amazing Technicolour Dreamcoat*, his primary passion during his youth and early adulthood was football.

Ben, Olly's younger twin, also enjoyed football and later said of their fraternal relationship, 'We were inseparable. Even though I'm ten minutes younger, I always felt like his big brother. If someone was being rough with him on the pitch, I'd sort it out.' The two clashed from time to time as youngsters but rancour would always be short-lived. 'Me and Ben were always close,' Olly told ITV2 in 2010. 'Two peas in a pod. If we ever had a row with each other, it never lasted more than three or four hours. Within an hour we'd be back, playing our computer games together.'

As a spectator, Olly's first big football match took place at Wembley Stadium in March 1996, just weeks away from his 12th birthday. A few months before England hosted the UEFA Euro '96 tournament, it was a friendly between England and Bulgaria. Olly was becoming a promising player at his new secondary school, Notley High in Braintree, which previously educated such notables as Leeroy Thornhill, keyboard player with rave pioneers The Prodigy, and the dancer and choreographer Louis Spence. Olly's enthusiasm and skill for the game of football ensured that he became the centre-forward of the school side. By the time he was 15, he even had a trial for Southend United.

For some in Essex, the league team to support is Southend United, or Colchester United, or maybe a London club like West Ham United. But Olly could not resist the appeal of a club further north. As a child, worshipping the skills of players like David Beckham, Eric Cantona and Roy Keane, he was already a fan of Manchester United FC, perhaps the dominant English football team of the past 20 years. The club has won the Premiership title a total of 19 times, including 12 times since 1992, and lifted the FA Cup Final trophy on 11 occasions. They even had a number-one hit record in 1994, 'Come On You Reds'. If pushed to nominate a second team he favours, he selects another team from the north-west of England. 'I'd probably say Wigan. There's something about them, they're really hometown. They're not vicious, they don't cause any problems, they just go about their business. Their fans kind of applaud what other teams do.'

In his late teens, between 2001 and 2003, Olly studied sport and recreation at Braintree College of Further Education, but some remember that his fondness for music was constantly breaking through even then. Anna Simon (who later became a tutor at the college) was a fellow student who would not be surprised by his subsequent breakthrough. 'He often entertained us with impromptu singing and dance, and was a charismatic entertainer back then,' she said.

Eventually, Olly played as a semi-professional in the reserve side for Witham Town FC, but still dreamed of Premier League stardom. 'My record was pretty good,' he recalled. 'I think I scored something like forty goals in twenty or thirty games.' He modelled himself on the Irish player Robbie Keane who, during Olly's time as a regular player, was one of the stars of Tottenham Hotspur. 'I like the fact Robbie could score goals but could really play as well,' said Olly, aware that teamwork and helping to create the goals, not just scoring them, is central to being a good player.

By 2006, Witham Town's reserve team was a treble-winning side and Olly would make the club's first team. But he would get no further in the world of soccer, unlike his teammate Cody McDonald, who would later be a striker for league sides Norwich City and (from 2011) Coventry City.

Witham Town reserves winger Matt Dean knew Olly from both on and off the pitch. They had been close mates ever since their ex-girlfriends had been best friends and he would harbour fond memories of some hedonistic nights out with both Murs twins in Chelmsford. 'We would watch Olly and Ben own the dance floor,' he said. 'They would be incredible.'

Kirk Setford was another of Olly's footballing friends of several years. They had played together for a Sunday team called the Howbridge Swifts and Kirk watched him develop some killer dance-floor moves at clubs in Witham, as well as accompany him abroad. 'When we went on a stag do in Amsterdam, he had the DJ trying to outdo him by playing different songs,' recalled Kirk. 'Every song the DJ played, Olly did a different dance and everyone was loving it.'

All the while, during his time as a centre-forward, Olly worked in nine-to-five jobs during the week. He had trained to be a fitness instructor but, when he discovered he did not relish the job, he followed in the footsteps of his mum Vicky-Lynn and worked as a recruitment consultant. For about four years, he worked at Prime Appointments in Witham's Newland Street. Again, according to its managing director, Robyn Holmes, his potential as a singer could not be silenced: 'He has sung for us in the past, at Christmas parties, and we always thought what a talented singer he was.' The sound of his singing was ever-present around the offices and, if he wasn't singing, he'd be listening to music.

By 2009, he was working as a customer advisor at Climate Energy Ltd in the same town's Freebournes Road. Here, he handled telephone calls from customers who were seeking advice on how to save energy in and around their homes. His boss was Tracy Baird. 'It was a pleasure working with Olly,' she said in the light of his success. 'We all miss his dance moves and his tremendous voice.'

Later, Olly reflected on his ordinary working life before *X Factor*. 'I had regular jobs, working nine-to-five like most people and earning the minimum wage. I worked in a jam factory and I worked in another factory, then call centres.' Working in the latter, he found himself selling kitchens, then mortgages. If work was unremarkable, he was relatively carefree. 'Me and my brother didn't really appreciate the money side of things and the pressure our parents were under. Being young lads, going out every weekend, we'd miss paying rent and stuff like that because we didn't know what was going on. We were just going out, splashing our money on drink, me and my mates playing football.' He later came to appreciate the sacrifices his parents made. 'Now I realise the stress – the mortgage, the bills – it mounts up. So it is very difficult and I'm sure they go through a lot.'

'It's always been his dream to be a pop star or a

professional football player,' said twin brother Ben in 2009. 'But as he got older, music took over. We used to watch *The X Factor* at home and I would say, "Why don't you just go on it?" But he didn't have the confidence to take the next step.'

In the spring of 2007, Olly finally mustered up the confidence to audition for the programme. Interestingly, in the light of his current status as an 'entertainer', his choice of song was the essence of fun, if not the greatest technical challenge for a budding singer. 'I Wanna Be Like You' was one of the most popular songs from the much-loved 1968 Disney animated feature *The Jungle Book*. His rendition was unsuccessful, neither good nor poor enough to be televised.

A year later, he tried a second time. This time, his song of choice was 'Last Request' by Paolo Nutini. Again, success proved elusive and his attempt would not be screened. 'Olly was very disappointed,' twin brother Ben would tell one newspaper. 'But I kept encouraging him to give it another go.'

Perhaps some regular singing experience in front of people would help. Olly's ambition to be a singer was growing day by day, albeit on a modest scale. Unlike the likes of Jessie J, Amy Winehouse and Katie Melua, he would not study at the Brit School in Croydon. Instead he began attending karaoke nights at his local pub in Witham, The George. 'It turned into a Sunday night thing. The place would get busy and it was obvious they were coming to see me.'

'Even then, he took everything in his stride,' sister Fay later marvelled. 'I remember seeing a poster in The George advertising a "Singalong with Olly Night". I couldn't believe it. He's not one to brag and, when I quizzed him about it, he was so laid back.'

Olly quickly became known as a versatile performer, with his repertoire encompassing covers of soul, funk and Motown standards, as well as approximations of Elvis Presley and Frank Sinatra. His repertoire had something for everyone, in short, and such was his popularity that The George's landlord, John Fisher, offered him regular gigs with guitarist friend, Jon Goodey. 'I was terrified,' said Olly, 'but thought why not. I had always enjoyed singing and it was a success.' As Small Town Blaggers, Murs and Goodey were paid £150 a night. 'We ended up being booked in lots of different pubs doing fifties and sixties theme nights,' said Olly. 'It was all word of mouth. They would be packed. I knew from then what I wanted to do.' Among their repertoire was one of Olly's favourites from childhood: The Proclaimers' 'I'm Gonna Be (500 Miles)'. 'It's one of them songs. As soon as you start playing it, it's such a big party song. The whole crowd would start singing it.'

Olly's subsequent spell in a group called F2K would lead to a friendship with singer Lara George. Their association would endure: in October 2010 they would sing together at the wedding of Olly's elder sister Fay.

Pub gigs, a few parties, a wedding or two – Olly was getting the taste for singing, dancing and performing. But money remained scarce and it was time for one or two reality checks from his family. First, his grandfather sat him down for a talk. 'He said, "What are you doing with your life? At your age I had a house, a wife, kids and a car. More importantly, I had a decent job. What have you got?"'

One subsequent family dinner brought things to a head. 'We did say he needed to concentrate on his job,' admitted his mum Vicky-Lynn in 2010. 'They all ganged up on me,' said Olly, 'saying I needed to get a proper job. I knew they were being realistic but it was sad because, after all the different jobs I'd done since I was sixteen, there I was finally doing something I loved.' He dearly hoped that he might be able to make a proper living out of his passion but the job of singing – just like any full-time job – takes patience, determination and a lot of hard work. And some luck too.

Maybe he'd have some good luck at a TV 'dream factory' near Bristol. In between his first two *X Factor* auditions, Olly Murs applied to appear on a daily game show, which had been a must-see for afternoon viewers since debuting on Channel 4 in October 2005. Noel Edmonds' *Deal or No Deal* was a game of chance and strategy. Contestants, faced with 22 sealed boxes containing mystery sums of money ranging from 1p to £250,000, had to eliminate each one until they were left with the last box: their prize. Every now and again, a figure called 'The Banker' would call Noel on a telephone and offer the contestant a sum of money, to which they would either say 'Deal' or 'No deal'.

Because *Deal or No Deal* was a programme where contestants might appear several times on screen before they got the chance to play the game, regular eagle-eyed viewers would come to recognise recurrent competitors. Olly featured on some 29 editions and would consequently be recognised in the street.

Olly was finally selected to play *Deal or No Deal* in an episode broadcast on the afternoon of Thursday, 13 December 2007. It was his first television appearance. His mum and dad had made him a special Good Luck card. It read, 'You only sit in the "crazy chair" once so make the most of it.' Olly was thrilled to meet Noel. 'An absolutely great guy,' he told his local paper, the *Braintree and Witham Times*. 'I think a lot of people criticise him but he is there for you and wants you to win.'

Watching the programme again, we can see a burgeoning star in the making. Olly flirts with fellow contestants, previews some dance moves on the set's Walk of Wealth and takes some risks. He went on the show to win some money for his unwell mum but, sadly, his efforts were not rewarded. Turning down the mystery banker's offer of some £22,000 at one point, he ended up with a paltry tenner. But Olly was not downhearted and Noel Edmonds, having no idea of what was round the corner, uttered some words which seem prophetic now. 'Every now and again we meet a special person. You do not have failure written over you.'

Olly was philosophical about his performance on a show that, after all, is so often down to pure chance. 'At the time winning the £10 note wasn't my highlight,' he recalled in 2011, 'but it's made me the person I am today. I've come out on the other side.'

Olly's efforts at conquering TV had hit a wall – and so had his days as a footballer, at least for now. In late 2008, the effects of an old injury on the football pitch led to him needing an operation. He had damaged one of the four ligaments in his knee during a game and so now underwent keyhole surgery. Unable to play soccer at all for five months, he used some of the money earned by Small Town Blaggers to spend some recovery time on the other side of the world.

Olly's trip travelling around Australia would be both 'an incredible adventure' and a directionless period of his life. He described it as a time 'when my life was at quite a low. I didn't know who I wanted to be, what I wanted to do.' But though he had no idea of where his future lay, he told MTV Australia in 2012 that it acted as a time of reflection and soul-searching for him: 'I just thought Australia was a great way out of the UK and a chance for me to rebuild some bridges and try and figure out where I'm gonna go with my life. I had three great months, came back and just felt really energised, like I could take on the world.'

He was on the verge of extending his stay but decided against it. From thousands of miles away, he had been keeping an eye on the 2008 series of the British *X Factor* and, specifically, one of its competing acts. They would fail to beat Alexandra Burke in the final but vocal quartet JLS showed that they might have the potential to outgrow the programme and to succeed in their own right. This they would do, in time selling out a tour and scoring number-one hits. For Louis Walsh, they turned out to be 2008's 'real winners. I gave them heart and soul, everything. I worked so hard for them.'

Olly returned to Britain, vowing to try for *X Factor* a third time in the spring of 2009. He told hardly anyone of his immediate plans at the time, but those close to him could tell there was a newfound determination in him. 'It was a turning point for him,' commented Ben Murs of his twin's time 'down under'. 'He grew up out there and his confidence bloomed. He went away a boy and came back a man.'

In the first week of May 2009, just one week before he turned 25 years old, Olly Murs was one of thousands who got up at the crack of dawn to travel to the O2 Arena near Greenwich in south-east London. He had never before made it past this first stage of *The X Factor* but, on this occasion, choosing Stevie Wonder rather than Disney or Paolo Nutini, coupled with a bit more experience, found favour with the programme's researchers and producers. He was invited to perform at Stage 2 of the audition process on 25 June in front of Simon Cowell, Louis Walsh, Cheryl Cole and Dannii Minogue. And this would be part of the new-look twist to the series – an audition in front of a live audience. It would be a baptism of fire and he would more than rise to the occasion.

There was little about Olly Murs' first 25 years that seemed in any way out of the ordinary. Even as a footballer, he was good enough to reach semi-professional level and regularly score goals for a local side but not to reach the national and international level of recognition achieved by heroes of his like David Beckham. Yet these unexceptional early years, spent both on the football pitch and in call-centre offices, were to give him an insight into hard work and perseverance. Any rewards were not easily won. His low-key career experiences would be invaluable for the life-changing events that lay ahead.

CHAPTER FOUR

TAKING
THE RISK

After passing Stage 2 of *The X Factor*, by auditioning in front of Louis Walsh, Dannii Minogue, Cheryl Cole and Simon Cowell, plus an excitable studio audience, Olly progressed to Stage 3 – what was known as 'bootcamp'. The judges had to reduce their long list of favoured candidates to just 24 – six acts in each of the four categories of Boys, Girls, Groups and Over-25s. Having turned 25 in mid-May, Olly had only just become eligible for the final category. 'The year I got in,' he would remember, 'I thought, "I'll be in the over-25s category now – it'll be easier".' But it turned out to be the hardest category there was.

Olly's bootcamp experience was broadcast to millions in late September 2009. His choice of song was Elton John's first ever British hit from 1971, 'Your Song'. He knew he had to give it everything. As with his June audition, he was engaging enough but, for Simon Cowell, something was missing. 'You know what's frustrating?' he admitted to his fellow panellists after Olly had left the stage. 'He was one of those guys who could've taken a risk. And instead he took the safe option. He could sing Elton John in his sleep.' The choice of song was a dilemma for any *X Factor* participant. Choose something too left field and you could alienate your audience. Opt for something familiar and you could bore them. What 'Your Song' failed to do for Simon Cowell, perhaps, was *entertain*.

Fortunately, Olly's potential remained strong and he was through to Stage 4, where he and the other successful competitors would sing for the mentor of their respective categories at their lavish home abroad. In his case, that meant jetting to Los Angeles and Simon's house. Cowell would pick three out of the remaining six to stay in the competition for the live finals back in London. The unsuccessful other three would also be jetting back to Britain but would be out of the contest.

X Factor co-executive producer Siobhan Greene had previously worked on *Stars in Their Eyes*. She revealed in 2012 why they flew the contestants halfway around the world to sing for their mentors at their homes. 'We wanted to do it a bit like "Lives of the Rich and Famous",' she said. The hopefuls could imagine that one day they might have the same sort of lives: "If I do really well, I could have a little piece of this!"'

Olly told series host Dermot O'Leary that being in the

competition was akin to being at Silverstone race track because he didn't know what lay round the next corner. And he knew the end could come at any minute. 'If it is a "no", it's back home to Essex, back home to my energy advising job.' He had lived the nine-to-five life long enough to know that, while his office job earned him some money, it did not give him the same level of excitement and enjoyment that singing was offering him. The question was, just how hard did he want this newfound career in the spotlight?

The judges' houses' footage was shown on *The X Factor* over the first weekend of October 2009, the same weekend that Simon celebrated his 50th birthday. Olly was shown standing by the pool at Cowell's LA house, singing to him and his long-time friend and associate, the 1980s popster Sinitta.

This time, he sang 'A Song for You', a ballad written by the American singer-songwriter Leon Russell in the early 1970s, but more recently recorded by the Canadian crooner Michael Bublé. One of the early couplets in the song could scarcely have been more appropriate for this stage of *X Factor*. Olly had indeed sung in front of thousands – ultimately, millions – during Stage 2. Now in Stage 4, he was in a more intimate environment, singing to his mentor at his Californian abode.

There were no crowds willing him on this time. Olly was tense as he stood in front of Simon, Sinitta and the show's technical crew, awaiting his fate of either success or oblivion. When he had finished, Simon admitted to Olly that his responsibility was to choose someone whom he thought could win the series final in December. How sure could you be of someone's potential? He soberly told Olly, 'You're a risk, it's as simple as that.' There then followed one of Simon's trademark never-ending pauses. Eventually, he spoke again. 'Sometimes I have to take risks. You're in.' Tearful with relief, Olly embraced Simon and promised, 'I'm gonna give it everything.'

Sinitta's connection with Simon dated back to the mid-1980s when his Fanfare record label had released her first hit, 'So Macho'. She told the *Sun* she had helped him to pick Olly as one of the three Over-25s finalists. 'We fought about Olly Murs. I knew he was a star. Simon wasn't sure but, the more he watched him, the more he started to get the Olly Factor!' Cowell was already convinced they had now chosen correctly. 'Everyone loves Olly,' he said. 'You meet him, you like him. He has the likeability factor and he's a natural entertainer.'

Olly may have been nervous in front of Simon and Sinitta but he'd been a sensation in front of thousands of people back in June. And that was what mattered in a pop career – engaging with large numbers confidently but being human with individuals.

Fighting against Olly for Simon's approval in the Over-25s category (and the approval of the other three judges too) were two other male singers who had stormed through their auditions. Aged 27, Danyl Johnson, a singing teacher from Reading, delivered a version of the Beatles' 'With a Little Help from My Friends', which

Cowell described as the best opening audition he had ever seen. Then there was 34-year-old Jamie 'Afro' Archer, whose audition performance of 'Sex on Fire' had helped to nudge the original version by Kings of Leon back into the top 10 of the singles chart.

The other three categories already had their front-runners. Much touted in Cheryl Cole's Boys camp was Joseph McElderry from South Shields in the north-east of England. Still just 18 years old, Joe had got as far as the bootcamp stage two years earlier in 2007 but had quit, feeling that he was too young to continue in the contest. Guiding the Girls, meanwhile, was Dannii Minogue. A strong contender there was Stacey Solomon from Dagenham in Essex. Stacey, a single mum who had just turned 20 years of age, had become the hit of bootcamp with what one newspaper summarised as a 'soulful voice and endless legs'.

But before the live finals even got underway, there was no denying which act was attracting most attention, much of it negative. The 17-year-old Dublin twins John and Edward Grimes had already led Cowell to brand them as 'vile, irritating creatures' and 'two of the most annoying people we have had on in a long time'. They were soon dubbed 'the Brothers Grim'. Louis Walsh was more positive though. They reminded him of Boyzone, the group he managed from the 1990s, who debuted on Irish TV with an embarrassing dance display but survived the experience and scored some of the biggest hits of the decade. 'Everybody said they weren't going to make it,'

Louis told the twins, 'but they did and there's a little bit of that with you guys.' He also called them 'the new Bros', fully aware that the Goss twin pop sensations of the late 1980s had attracted devotion, or flak, but almost never indifference.

Louis would mentor the Grimes brothers in the Groups category. He knew that, in pop music and in television terms, annoying the viewing public a little was a sure-fire way of holding their attention. Take out anyone infuriating and *The X Factor* risked having a succession of good singers with similar personalities. The need to keep the public interested/irked was paramount. In reality-TV entertainment, the only sin is to be boring.

It was important to find strong newcomers – ones with big personalities – rather than bring back middling pop figures to have another go. These competitions were about discovering stars, not reviving them. Ex-members of One True Voice (who came second on *Popstars: The Rivals* in 2002) and S Club Juniors came close to being short-listed on *The X Factor* in 2009 but did not progress further. There was concern at the number of 'recycled' acts, ones who had already achieved minor success without becoming household names, or familiar faces from other TV talent shows. Someone like Olly Murs, with no obvious track record in the music industry, was exactly the sort of figure Cowell and his team might be looking for.

Olly and the other lucky *X Factor* finalists would be house sharing during the weeks of the show's live finals. Home would be a specially designated six-bedroom house based in Golders Green, North London. Worth an estimated £6 million, its other features included a gym, a 'media room' with computer games and a 63" plasma TV, and a suspended walkway that extended out from the kitchen on to a landscaped garden.

The 12 remaining acts in the contest had moved in on Monday, 5 October 2009, five days before the live finals began on TV. Any floor-to-ceiling windows were papered over to keep out the lenses of the paparazzi. But once young fans became aware of its existence, it became common for them to gather outside. School head teachers were asked by the programme's executives to try to stop pupils from going near it but youngsters persisted in hanging around. One 12-year-old fan suggested the obsession was one of curiosity rather than out-and-out fandom. 'I don't think they're proper celebrities,' she said. 'But they're on TV at the moment and I know who they are, so I wanted to see what they're like in real life.'

By late October, when schools were on a half-term break, the press were reporting that neighbouring residents were tiring of the noise. Some young visitors were showing up as early as 6.30 a.m. and leaving litter around the area. The Chinese Ambassador, Madam Fu Ying, lived nearby and was reported as having complained to the Foreign Office about the constant commotion. A spokesperson for the Chinese Embassy – who had had the property since 1959 – confirmed that a complaint had been made after girls had defaced the intercom at the Ambassador's front door and the border fence of her property with declarations of love for both Olly and fellow contestant Lloyd Daniels.

John and Edward were soon in hot water too: a story circulated that, when two teenagers flashed their breasts at them, they responded by gripping their crotches in a Michael Jackson fashion. This led to them being banned from signing autographs or having any other contact with fans. The last straw for the residents was a fans' 'serenade' to Olly, which took place at 2.30 a.m. Police patrols increased around the property and a fence was erected, as plans were made to relocate the *X Factor* house to another area of London for the next series.

But the clamour of fans outside the house was an interesting challenge for the stars of the future inside. How would they cope with the attention, and with the constant requests for a smile and a kiss to be blown? Despite an 8.30 p.m. curfew for the house's temporary occupants, the truly persistent who hung around longer and later might be rewarded with a friendly wave. It was soon reported that Olly was especially happy to acknowledge and engage with such fans. When in the public eye, you don't always get to choose when and how you encounter the people who keep you there. You may be having a bad day as a celebrity but it pays to be cheery and engaging, not grumpy or aloof. Especially when there's a competition to be won. 'We're not there to make friends,' Olly would later say. 'We're there to win the show.'

Female fans outside the property weren't Olly's only admirers. Inside, rival Danyl said the best-looking guy in the house had to be Olly. 'He's a true man's man. He is always walking about just in his pants.' As Danyl, Jamie and Olly were all sharing the same room, things could get tense in such close proximity. Reports circulated saying that there was a no-sex rule in the house, which could be frustrating, especially for the slightly older contenders. 'We aren't allowed any female visitors,' explained Olly. 'We all cuddle. But it can be a bit too much having all these beautiful girls hug you. You're like, "Oh God, I give up."'

An endless stream of stories from inside the house would seep into the gossip columns of the newspapers that autumn. Inevitably, many of them centred round the teenage twins John and Edward. Had they eaten all the food in the kitchen? Were they the source of an infestation of head lice? That one was never confirmed but it underlined their role in the contest – and in the house – as larger-than-life and all-purpose cartoon irritants.

There were tensions between other house occupants. Olly was reportedly finding Danyl's obsession with tidiness something of a strain. Jamie would claim to one Sunday newspaper the reason for Olly's tendency to wander around the house in just his undies: 'He said it's because he used to play football and everyone would just walk around the dressing room like that.' And by the end of the series, Olly and Danyl were, according to some reports, barely speaking to each other.

Assuming these relatively minor disagreements are genuine, it should be remembered that these were strangers, both professionally and personally, having to live and work under enormous pressure and a media spotlight for weeks on end. In the circumstances, it's hardly surprising that a few petty irritations surfaced. For each of these contestants, including Olly Murs, every day in the *X Factor* house during the autumn of 2009 would be a whirl of excitement, energy and nerves. And from their sixth day of living there – Saturday, 10 October – their performances on *The X Factor* would be broadcast to the nation live.

CHAPTER FIVE

THE ENTERTAINER

Every autumn, the Saturday night live finals of *The X Factor* would transfix millions of viewers tuned to ITV1. Late 2009 would be no exception. As before, during each programme, the finalists would battle it out in front of the judges, studio audience and viewers at home by performing cover versions of familiar and much-loved songs. Most editions would be themed, opening up a classic artist's back catalogue or choosing a musical genre ('Disco', 'Big Band', 'Rock'). Occasionally, there would be a broader theme like 'Halloween'. After each competitor had performed, each judge would comment on how they thought they had fared. Then the public was asked to vote on which act they would most like to see return to sing again the following week.

On Sunday nights, the two acts with the fewest number of public votes were called back to the stage to participate in a live 'sing-off'. Based on that performance, the four judges would decide between them which act should stay and which one should be eliminated. The unsuccessful competitor would leave with immediate effect, while the survivor and the other remaining contestants began feverish preparations for the next weekend's battle.

Performers would not have long to make an impact. Most of their renditions were edited adaptations of a popular hit (usually no more than two to two and a half minutes in length). There were advantages and disadvantages to singing shorter versions of songs. They were required to sing less of a song but, at the same time, to make an impact very quickly and make their version of a song count. Overall, finalists were expected to be as versatile and flexible as possible. It would not do to only excel at one style of music, as most of the true greats of pop have dipped their toes into many different genres.

In the week leading up to the first televised live finals, the five most favoured acts were either Simon's acts in the Over-25s category (Olly, Danyl, Jamie) or Dannii's ones in the Girls shortlist (young Welsh singer Lucie Jones and Essex's Stacey Solomon). 'Dannii and Simon know they are in pole position to end up on top,' one show source whispered to the press. 'Louis is gutted to get the Groups again. He's even had to resort to John and Edward Grimes in an attempt to get some attention back from the others.' Louis accepted that the chances of his acts winning was slim and acknowledged that Simon's

Over-25s acts had maturity on their side. 'They've all been round the block a fair bit,' he said. 'They've all got more experience than mine.'

Olly Murs may not have had oodles of professional 'experience' but he knew enough to know his strengths and limitations. 'The others were better singers,' he said of those who were dropped after the auditions at the judges' houses, but emphasised, 'I think that we were the best entertainers.' He did not take his finals placing for granted. 'I don't see myself as someone who can win it. I am just taking each week as it comes. If the public like me, I will just do what I can.' And he remained realistic about the ferocious competition facing him. 'There is so much talent here,' he said, simply.

He knew there was an extra ingredient that set him apart from much of the opposition – his dancing skills. Yet, just as he had never received vocal training, his dancing was all self-taught – the result of observing the music idols of his youth. 'Anything I've ever done is off the cuff. I've never rehearsed anything in my life. The stuff you have seen is from me watching Michael Jackson and Justin Timberlake, and putting my own thing on it.'

In addition to his skills and personality, he had some secret lucky charms just in case. These were three bracelets – two made of leather (which he had acquired on his Australian break) and one of beads. The beaded bracelet was given to him by an ex-girlfriend called Keli Flower. 'Her mum said, if I was to wear them this year, I'd be very successful on a TV show, singing. I've kept them on ever since, through all my auditions, and they seem to be giving me good luck.'

The first of *The X Factor* 2009 live finals took place on Saturday, 10 October. The theme was the work of Robbie Williams and the boy band that spawned him in the 1990s – Take That. Williams himself, who had sensationally quit the group in 1995 before embarking on an even bigger solo career with hits like 'Angels' and 'Let Me Entertain You', was to perform as a guest artist on the Sunday night edition, while admitting that he was nervous about his live TV comeback. But he was encouraging to several of the competitors, notably Stacey Solomon ('Stacey's great, I want one, I think every home should have one') and her fellow Essex contemporary. 'I love Olly Murs,' enthused Robbie. 'I want him to be my mate.' Before long, others would start to compare the two, among them Neil Fox, aka Dr Fox, the radio DJ who had been one of the judges on *Pop Idol*. 'Olly's my favourite,' he said. 'He reminds me of Robbie Williams with his cheeky-chappie appeal. He's smiling and having a laugh. Above all, he's a real entertainer.'

It's striking that most of those who would shine across the series chose a Robbie song. John and Edward attempted 'Rock DJ'. Joe McElderry covered the more reflective 'No Regrets'. And Olly Murs's Robbie selection was 'She's the One', which he sang wearing a white Fred Perry shirt. Written by Karl Wallinger for his group World Party in 1997, Robbie's reworking of the song had reached number one in the UK in 1999. But how did

Olly cope with the pressures of singing to an audience including Robbie himself? Easy: 'I just stared into his eyes and sang.'

The panel's response was unanimously positive. 'Everybody on the crew wants to be your friend, not just Robbie Williams!' cried Dannii Minogue. Cheryl Cole recognised that Olly had been 'stomach-wrenchingly nervous' but had 'pulled it back by the end of the song'. They acknowledged that Olly had sung very well but all took time out to note that his likeability and charisma had been equally important. All four saw this in Olly and none more so than the man sitting at the far right-hand side of the judges' table: 'You've got to put this into perspective. Six months ago, you were selling electricity for a living – you've had no experience. Coming on this stage, you're singing a Robbie Williams song with Robbie sitting next door. You remind me of Robbie. You've got this humility about yourself. Robbie knows he's not the best singer in the world but he admits it. He's a brilliant entertainer. And you've got that charm about you, Olly.'

The audience whooped loudly in agreement. Simon Cowell finished his appraisal with the words, 'I think you did very well. Well done.'

An immensely proud Murs family were present at the first live final to see Olly in action and cheer him on. 'It was all a bit manic,' said his mum, Vicky-Lynn. 'After the show we had about half an hour with him but there were so many people wanting photos with him. We've never experienced anything like it before.' His football-playing pal Matt Dean cited his grounded self-confidence as part of his appeal. 'He always performs with a smile on his face and he is so down-to-earth. I think he will always stay that way. He loves his music, his football and his family.'

The X Factor's resident vocal coach Yvie Burnett was most impressed by Olly. He was a fast learner and willing to listen to advice. 'He's progressing so much vocally,' she said of him, 'and he's doing it so quickly.' Brian Friedman, who advised on choreography, believed that Witham's rising star was the 'most accomplished' of any of the finalists. 'I think Olly will win,' he predicted. 'He's got this charm, this charisma that the public really seems to gravitate towards, and he can handle calming it down and taking it in, so it's the best of both worlds – and he's got the personality.'

But Friedman warned viewers to watch out for John and Edward Grimes, the wildcard act of the series that many were already starting to love to hate. 'The boys are totally insane to watch in rehearsals – but they have a huge fan base. They are so bad that they are good. I enjoy working with them on their set – it's so theatrical and over the top.'

There were other contenders for this *X Factor* title. Dannii Minogue felt that Joe McElderry would attract the girls' votes and that many would be besotted by Stacey and her 'amazing voice' but also drew attention to 'adorable' Olly: 'A slow burner if you ask me.' Cheryl Cole, on the other hand, expressed concern that he might need to have a higher profile if he was to survive to the week of the grand final. 'I'm worried about Olly,' she told the *Sunday Mirror*. 'He is kind of not happening at the moment but one to watch out for. He's a dark horse and all the girls love him.'

A few professional critics were, at least for now, less kind. After the first live shows, the *Sun*'s TV reviewer Ally Ross wrote that, regardless of Olly's 'likeability factor', there was no sign of 'the sing-in-tune-ability factor'. In *The Times*, its TV critic Caitlin Moran pointed out that the 'ham-like Essex singer' was 'possibly the only singer working at the moment whose name rhymes with "polymers"'.

More common, though, was the view expressed by Louis Walsh, who regarded Olly as 'the likeable guy next door. You are a talent.' It was an endorsement which drew attention to the man's undeniable star quality and recognised he was rooted in the real world – a world that viewers and fans could relate to. He would appreciate stardom but would not take it for granted.

For the second weekend, Louis would be absent for the saddest of reasons, namely the untimely death of former Boyzone member Stephen Gately, aged just 33. As their former manager, he would be attending the funeral. As a result, he would miss a performance from special-guest artist Whitney Houston (another artist now sadly missing from the music world), as well as an airing of fellow judge Cheryl Cole's new single, 'Fight for This Love' – her debut as a solo artist after seven years as one-fifth of Girls Aloud. But though absent from the *X Factor*'s studios in Wembley, Louis Walsh did not shrink from giving his views on the week's songs and singers. And he deplored Simon's choice of song for Olly.

'A Fool in Love' dated from 1960 and was the very first hit in the USA for Ike and Tina Turner. The song had never reached the British charts and, though Tina would re-record the song for the biopic movie *What's Love Got to Do With It* in 1993, it was generally less well known than the duo's 'River Deep Mountain High' and 'Nutbush City Limits', or her later solo smashes like 'The Best' or 'Private Dancer'. Covering a relatively unknown song was a risk on a high-profile show like *The X Factor*. The theory is that an audience feels comfortable with famous songs and could react coolly to something less familiar. But if a contestant injected an 'obscure' song with sufficient personality, they might stand a chance of making that song their own.

Olly had been urged by guest mentor Whitney Houston to give the song a 'Tina-esque performance' and the three panellists physically present were as impressed with him as they had been the previous week. 'All of us fell under your spell,' said Dannii. 'You absolutely smashed it,' agreed Cheryl. Simon thought it a step up, and then some. 'It was fun, it was different, it wasn't what we'd previously seen, which was karaoke – it was original. That was in a different league.' And he couldn't resist a cheeky jibe at his fellow judges. 'And this is why all the contestants want to be mentored by me.' The absent Louis remained unmoved by the song, if supportive of the singer. Reacting on the social-networking site Twitter, he wrote, 'It was totally the wrong song choice by Simon. But I do really love Olly.'

Week three was Big Band week. Olly tackled 'Bewitched', the song which, in instrumental form, introduced the US TV fantasy sitcom of the 1960s. His confidence was blossoming considerably. He didn't just sing the song. He adlibbed greetings at the start and end, respectively: 'Good evening, ladies' (to the two accompanying dancers wearing mini witches' hats) and 'Thank you' to the audience.

Back on the panel after his enforced absence, Louis was happier with 'Bewitched' than with 'A Fool in Love'. 'I like the fact you didn't pick a predictable song. You're here for a long, long time.' 'One classy big-band performance,' was Dannii's view. 'Every week, you're coming into your own,' she said. Once again, Simon was more elaborate and snuck in a quip at the expense of the two female panellists. 'I know what it's like working with two witches.' After assuring everyone he was joking, he continued to Olly, 'To make big band work, you've got to have style, you've got to have charisma and you've got to have confidence. And you scored on all three.'

Olly was doing extremely well. But the glare of publicity, which arrived in the participants' lives so suddenly and rudely, could be overwhelming. Olly found the scrutiny and pressure almost too much to bear. He later revealed he was close to quitting after these first three weeks. 'I felt out of my depth because there were a lot of other acts who had stronger voices. Then I got a bit complacent about being there and wasn't performing as well as I should. I had a lot of conversations with Simon. He told me to remember my first audition. I'm so glad I listened to him.'

Next came Rock Week in week four. Guest mentor Jon Bon Jovi put the remaining finalists through their paces on how to perform rock songs. Olly's choice of song was John Lennon and Paul McCartney's 'Come Together', one of the last recordings made by The Beatles in 1969 as part of their classic LP *Abbey Road*. A recurring opinion shared by all four judges was Olly's progression. He was improving every single week, always learning. And when he sailed through to the last eight in the contest, it meant that now, whether he won or lost the series, he would be part of the upcoming spin-off *X Factor* live tour of Britain, due to begin in February 2010. There would be no shortage of his screaming fans turning up for those dates. Every week, Olly Murs' profile was rising further and further – and what's more, he was about to make his recording debut too.

CHAPTER SIX

SURVIVING
THE SING-OFF

It was eerily fitting that the first hit single to involve Olly Murs was a cover of a Michael Jackson hit. He had been a devoted fan of the 'King of Pop' since childhood, when Jacko songs like 'Billie Jean', 'Thriller', 'Bad' and 'Black or White' were always on the radio. Plus, in an extraordinary coincidence, it just so happened that Michael's death, at the age of just 50, was announced to the world on Thursday, 25 June 2009, only a few hours after Olly's breakthrough *X Factor* live audition had been taped.

'You Are Not Alone', written by R. Kelly and originally a number-one hit for Jackson in 1995, would not be a solo Olly single. It was a charity-single remake by the *X Factor* Finalists. Recorded in October 2009, proceeds of the remake would go to the Great Ormond Street Hospital for Children in central London. The decision to release a charity record had come about due to the huge success of the previous year's finalists recording a version of Mariah Carey's 'Hero' in aid of Help for Heroes. 'We decided we wanted to do something annually on the show to help good causes,' said Simon Cowell. 'This year we chose to work with Great Ormond Street to help raise funds for their incredible work.'

The finalists' version of 'You Are Not Alone' was recorded at Abbey Road Studios in London's St. John's Wood. The studios have been home to numerous legendary recordings by Cliff Richard, The Beatles, Pink Floyd, Oasis, Radiohead and, in 2009, Leona Lewis's second album, *Echo*. On 15 November 2009, the day before it became available to buy as a download, the finalists performed it live on the *X Factor* Sunday results show. Like Jackson's original version, the charity cover would reach number one, selling nearly 200,000 copies in its first week on sale.

The X Factor charity single was a rare moment of unity – a moment when participants and judges rested their competitive streak. Mostly, the series was a maelstrom of ferocious rivalry – one of the reasons why it continued to be so popular. Indeed, part of the key to the series' success lay in its two-tier battle. Not only were the acts in fierce competition but the series pitted their mentors against each other. The mentors wanted their acts to win so that *they* could win. 'It's the same as the contestants,' said Olly. 'The judges want to win. Simon is the most competitive man you could ever meet and he wants to win the show every year.'

In the first five series, between 2004 and 2008, Simon had guided two winners to victory – Steve Brookstein (2004) and Leona Lewis two years later. His rival panellists had one winning act each – Louis with Shayne Ward (2005), Dannii with Leon Jackson (2007) and Cheryl with Alexandra Burke in 2008.

With four weeks of live finals over and with audiences nudging 16 million viewers, Olly was looking like a potential winner. According to odds issued by the bookmakers William Hill as to who would win the series, he was 5/2 favourite to triumph. Joe was close behind with odds of 7/2, while even John and Edward (by now popularly known as Jedward) had gone from being rank outsiders (50/1) to contenders (10/1). There were now just six weeks to the series finals.

Olly was constantly being reminded of the gulf between this dreamworld of stardom and the reality of the ordinary life he had previously known. It was a bizarre situation but it had its own kind of reassurance – as long as you retained your sense of humour. Text messages from his long-time mates would arrive, taking the mickey out of his misty-eyed reactions to Simon's comments on live TV. 'I'm standing in front of Simon Cowell,' was Olly's defence, 'and he is changing my life.' It was hard to stay stiff-upper-lipped in the circumstances.

The fifth week was Movie Week and, for the second week running, Olly plumped for a song recorded by the Fab Four. Unlike 'Come Together', 'Twist and Shout' was not a Beatles song as such but had appeared on their

1963 debut LP *Please Please Me*, having been recorded in just one studio take. The song only belatedly became part of a movie soundtrack: in 1986, the Beatles' version featured in the John Hughes comedy *Ferris Bueller's Day Off*, about a teenager and his friends who skip the routines of school for thrills in the big city. At one point, Ferris (played by Matthew Broderick) winds up as the star of the city's parade and proceeds to mime to 'Twist and Shout', causing a sensation in the process.

The choice of song, however, split the judges. In fact, Simon was the only one of the four who had no reservations about it – and he was Olly's mentor in any case. The others were less convinced, especially Louis. 'Olly, I'm not blaming you. I think Simon picked a really silly song for a great singer.' While the boos continued to ring out, Dannii wondered if Olly fully believed in his song choice and Cheryl felt he was singing a lot of retro songs.

Simon was having none of it though and nor was the rest of the crowd: 'Unfortunately, guys, the audience is speaking. Louis, as for your comment about this being a "silly song", it was one of the Beatles' biggest hits.' By now he was virtually drowned out by the cheering and the outbreak of an 'Olly Olly Olly' chant that would grow louder in the weeks to come. But Simon still wasn't done. 'You've all been quite mean tonight. He put on a great show. It's En-ter-tainment.' To Olly, he ended with the words, 'You were fantastic.'

Olly later revealed that he had his own doubts about

'Twist and Shout'. 'As the series went on,' he later told the *Mail on Sunday*, 'I was taking it more and more seriously. I wasn't sure about "Twist and Shout".' But Simon Cowell was the voice of reason and support. He said, 'Olly, trust me. It's going to be great.' Sure enough, the run-through of the song in the rehearsal worked, as did the performance on TV. Simon's instinct, once again, was right.

'The thing about Simon,' Olly considered later, 'is that he really does know his stuff. The tweaks he's made on my songs – in my head I was thinking, "I'm not sure about this," but then every time it worked. I mean, the man's loaded, isn't he? You don't get that far without knowing a thing or two. I'm very happy to have him in my corner.' But then Simon believed in Olly's potential and returned the compliment. 'Olly deserves to win. He is consistently good, he has a wonderful personality and I genuinely believe in him. It's not just because he is in my group – not at all.' He also suggested Joe McElderry as someone who could rival Olly in the final, even though Cheryl was Joe's actual mentor.

It was on the *X Factor*'s weekly sister show, *The Xtra Factor* (screened on ITV2 immediately after the close of the main show on ITV1), where it became clear that it wasn't just Simon who rated Olly. In a secret ballot held in mid-November, for which all four judges were asked to predict a winner and put their choices in a box, both Cheryl and Louis chose Olly. 'They think Olly's the most likely winner,' said a programme source. 'It'll be tough for their own acts to take but it's the truth.'

'There's nothing fake about him,' said Louis, who felt that Olly belonged in the grand tradition of pop male icons like Gary Barlow and Will Young, with the added bonus of having the dance moves of Jamiroquai's frontman Jay Kay. 'He's the boy next door who absolutely loves music. He does all those silly dances but that's him – it's not put on.' Previous winner Leona Lewis predicted great things for Olly, especially if he 'capitalises on that Robbie Williams vibe he's got'. Even those working for other Saturday night TV shows couldn't resist backing him – Alesha Dixon, then a judge on the BBC's rival reality-TV show *Strictly Come Dancing*, called him the 'most charismatic' contestant. Other contestants were generous with praise. Sometimes it wasn't purely about his talent. 'He's just the most genuine person,' said Lucie Jones. 'He's got a kind heart and he cares for people.'

Guest mentors offered plenty of encouragement too. In week six, Brian May and Roger Taylor of Queen helped Olly tackle their 1979 hit paean to hedonism, 'Don't Stop Me Now'. Uncertain that Olly was a born rock singer, guitarist May advised him to take inspiration from his late lamented bandmate Freddie Mercury and to 'put his whole body into it' when performing the song. May and drummer Taylor were duly impressed with the result, which began as a slow ballad and built up, only switching into a rock number after the first chorus. 'You're the best performer we have in the show, by far,' was Dannii Minogue's response. 'You always entertain,' said Simon. 'You always give it a hundred per cent.' Then, realising this didn't sound quite spectacular enough, he upped his figure: 'Every single time, you give it a hundred and fifty per cent.'

The only hint of Olly criticism seemed to come from his own family and, even then, it seemed to be a generational, tongue-in-cheek doubt. His grandmother Eileen took a dim view of how he dressed sometimes. 'There have been loads of occasions when [she] has said to him, "Those trousers are a bit tight." He's like, "Nan, that's the fashion!"' He was more upset when one of his beloved Manchester United squad gave support to one of his rivals. 'I was distraught when Wayne Rooney picked Danyl to win. I want him to know I'm a massive United fan.'

All in all, Olly was praised far more than attacked but the pressures on having to deliver every single week could be considerable. How did he cope? In a way, he would already have been used to it, albeit on a smaller scale. As a footballer, every Saturday (and sometimes midweek too) he would have faced some tough talking from the team's manager and coach, not to mention the cheers (and maybe boos) from both the Witham supporters and the fans of the opposing team.

As a football-team member, he would have been aware that, while he wanted to stand out on the pitch, it was ultimately about teamwork. And *The X Factor*, while there could only be one winner, required everyone involved (contestants, mentors) to pull together and give their best, to make the most entertaining show possible every single time. 'I always look at things like football teams,' he would later say. 'In any business, you have to refresh. No one is bigger than the club.'

In week seven, Olly looked vulnerable. His rendition of George Michael's 1996 chart-topper 'Fastlove' was uncharacteristically shaky, his vocal a touch flat, though still undeniably entertaining and compelling. 'Broad appeal', 'Everything about Olly Murs is real' and 'You are turning into a fearless performer' were some of the comments from the panel. 'Olly, I wanna have your babies!' was another response, though this came from an audience member.

The viewing public was suddenly less sure. For the first time, Olly was in the bottom two of the weekly vote and had to return for the Sunday night sing-off against the most divisive act of the series – John and Edward Grimes. Jedward had already caused an upset the previous week, surviving that week's sing-off against Lucie Jones. The panel chose spectacle over raw talent. Lucie was to go. Jedward were to stay. At least for the time being.

The panel knew by now that, although the public always claimed to favour talent, a successful TV show should always get the public talking. And sometimes what got the public talking was something sensationally bad, something that was memorable for all the wrong reasons, even something that was simply infuriating. This is not the sole explanation as to why Jedward survived so long on *X Factor* but they were like nothing else on the show and people continued to want to see them. Defying Simon

Cowell's continuing denouncements of their act, viewers voted in droves to ensure they kept returning to fight another day.

Three years after her *X Factor* win, singer Leona Lewis accepted that the ethos of the programme had broadened. It was no longer *only* a singing contest. 'When I was on the show in 2006, it was only about the singing,' she said. 'I can't believe how much it has changed. It's not just about singing really well anymore. It's a TV show and they want their entertainment value.' And some newspaper critics felt that the search for 'entertainment' over 'technical ability' was itself stuck in the past. One critic summed up Olly Murs as sharing the 'old-fashioned' philosophy of *The X Factor* itself: 'a sort of song-and-dance man in the Michael Barrymore mould, without Barrymore's range.'

For Olly, being in the bottom two against Jedward would be hell. Nerve-racking enough performing in front of the viewing and voting millions, it was worse knowing that the panel could eliminate him on a whim. 'Trust me, it was horrible, it really was,' he told one reporter. There was none of the relief of learning your fate was safe. 'You're just hoping your name comes out and, when your name doesn't come out, your heart just fills. You're like, "Oh God."'

Eventually, though, Jedward's luck (and some saw it purely as luck) would run out. Having at least had the opportunity to use their OTT personalities to cover outlandish pop songs like 'Ghostbusters', it's hard to make Boyzone's 'No Matter What' sound wacky, no matter how tall your hair might be. While Louis loyally backed the twins, Simon, Dannii and Cheryl favoured Olly, whose sensitive treatment of Eric Clapton's 'Wonderful Tonight' would put him through.

Relief for Olly. 'There's no way you deserved to be in the bottom two,' Louis insisted. But sometimes life isn't fair and, as Simon noted, Olly faced his sing-off challenge against Jedward with maturity and level-headedness. 'No sulking, no complaining, you got on with it,' he congratulated him.

So it wasn't the end for Olly, but nor was it curtains for Jedward. Louis, who soon took them on as clients, felt there were almost limitless possibilities for the twins. 'Hair endorsements! Panto, TV, lots of things.' Irksome as they could be, Louis mourned their departure. From now on, it was just another talent show. 'You knew what was going to happen – everyone was going to come out and sing well.' It wasn't just a singing contest. 'You need spectacle. We didn't manufacture them, they manufactured themselves.'

'Nothing ever affected them,' marvelled Olly of the much maligned twins. 'They just got on with it.' But he wondered if they might have been less the targets of ridicule and hatred if cameras had been installed in the *X Factor* house to witness the behind-the-scenes shenanigans. 'They never had a bad mood. They never took criticism to heart. They'd poke fun at themselves too. They never took themselves seriously and it's a shame some members of the public did and booed them.'

Ultimately, Louis believed that talent was only one aspect of a superstar and that it wasn't necessarily the most important. 'Ambition, drive and work ethic are almost more important. The most successful artists are not necessarily the best singers. Madonna and Robbie [Williams] have got great drive but, if you bring them in here and get them to sing a cappella, it's not gonna be great.' In addition, any budding performer seeking mainstream success required a platform, a good management company and PR, plus the help of press, radio and television.

But real vacancies for new stars were at a premium, even via the high-profile platform of *X Factor*. 'We've had Leona, Alexandra Burke and JLS,' argued Louis, but he emphasised, 'Very few people have star quality.' Asked if he felt any responsibility for the fate of performers like Steve Brookstein and Leon Jackson, whose time in the spotlight was fleeting, he said no. 'Because they get one chance. This show is a platform for people who have got talent and, if they use it properly, it's just a chance. They're not all going to be stars.'

Olly Murs only had one chance. But he was certainly making it last.

CHAPTER SEVEN

BACK STORIES

A contestant's backstory (often disparagingly called a 'sob story') is an integral part of the TV talent show in the 21st century. To take part in any high-profile TV series is not a decision to take lightly. Why do so many people apply? Is it an opportunity for them to prove themselves? Some say they are trying to overcome some kind of adversity in their life, whether it's a disadvantage of some sort, or overcoming an illness, or reacting to difficult circumstances. For them, it's about creating their own personal victory, whether or not they end up winning or becoming famous.

By the end of October 2009, Olly Murs had become a weekly fixture on *The X Factor*. Many were impressed with his singing and dancing skills, and found him likeable, but the reasons behind his drive and motivation mostly remained a mystery.

Then it transpired that his mum Vicky-Lynn was not in good health. Five years earlier, she had been forced to give up her job, suffering from what was described as a 'debilitating ME-type virus'. She found she was constantly exhausted and had considerable difficulty eating.

One of Olly's goals, if he were to win *The X Factor*, was to spend the money on finding the best doctor possible to find out more information about the mysterious illness and to help her convalesce and recover. In the meantime, she was able to attend the *X Factor* live shows every Saturday and Sunday night, on condition that she rested properly for the remainder of the week. 'Because ME is so complex – everyone gets it differently – she hasn't been diagnosed properly yet,' Olly told the *Daily Mail* in 2010. 'But we've got our fingers crossed that she'll be OK.'

Otherwise, as far as the mass viewing public was concerned, there was no obvious test for him yet – nothing in his way that might prevent him from committing to the show. But this was about to change.

On 1 November 2009, the *Sunday Mirror* reported that Olly's twin brother Ben was soon to marry his fiancée Amy. The church wedding was due to take place in the Essex town of Chelmsford, to be followed by a reception for 100 guests at a Grade-II listed venue just outside the town. But the date chosen for the wedding could scarcely have been more problematic from an *X Factor* finalist's point of view. Saturday, 5 December was the date of the show's semi-final. Even though the live show would be broadcast in the evening, four hours after the 3 p.m.

ceremony, the programme's bosses said it would be impossible for Olly to attend the wedding, as it would clash with vital pre-show rehearsals.

Olly and Ben had been close throughout their childhoods, seeing each other every day and night without fail. Ben had only moved out of the family home in Witham six months before, in April 2009, just after Olly had returned from Australia. It was the first period that the two brothers had not lived under the same roof – and it was tough. 'I suffered from homesickness for the first few months,' said Ben. 'We'd never been this far apart. We grew in the same womb.'

'My wedding day will be the biggest day of my life,' Ben would say. 'And, of course, I want my twin brother there. But the only way he will be at my wedding will be if he's voted off the show. And I don't want that either.'

Was there a third option? It seemed there might be. It was a given that Olly couldn't possibly attend the wedding reception. But surely he could attend the ceremony at the church? Ben had a plan: 'My dream would be for Simon Cowell to let Olly take the day off from the show for me and my wife. Even if he just turned up for the ceremony then got back to the studio in time to perform, it would be the best wedding present we could ask for.'

Assuming he would still be in the competition by early December, Olly faced a tricky dilemma. What was more important – attending a family wedding or pursuing his career? You might argue it's a no-brainer. Why bother with some silly TV show when one of your own flesh and blood is tying the knot? But signing a contract stating that *The X Factor* was his job (at least until his elimination) effectively committed Olly to the show.

In a sense, a showbiz figure cancelling a high-profile engagement for a family wedding is of no interest to the public at large. Prioritising *The X Factor* over everything else was an early example of what faced contestants if they embarked on a show-business career. To make fame last, no matter how it might look on TV or in the papers, takes hard work, and entertaining the public is the top priority in an entertainer's life.

There had been a precedent for missing a live round of *X Factor* without having to leave the contest – Diana Vickers had suffered a bout of laryngitis in the 2008 series and been permitted leave for that week to recover. Ill-health was one thing. A clash of engagements, though, was another matter entirely.

Ben had first realised back in September 2009 that *The X Factor* might collide with his wedding, which had been 18 months in preparation. Back then, Olly had called him from Simon Cowell's home in Los Angeles to warn him there would be a problem. 'I told him to concentrate on the show,' he told the *Sunday Mirror* later. 'This is his chance. I told him, "You can't be in two places at once. Do what you've got to do."' At least Ben had a Plan B. An alternative best man – Tommy Bradley, a close friend of both twins – would step in if Olly could not make it to the ceremony. 'Olly kept saying sorry,' Ben revealed. 'But

I told him not to apologise and to go for it.' Wedding planners were on standby just in case Olly was able to make it after all. But if not, Olly would be kept up to date. 'We'll be in touch by phone throughout the day,' assured Ben. 'We may even put the wedding on speakerphone so he can hear our vows.'

The preparations for Ben's marriage to Amy had somewhat overshadowed how much attention he could pay to Olly's progress on television every week. Unlike other family members, he had not been at *The X Factor's* Wembley studios to cheer on his brother. He denied there was any rift with Olly. 'I love my brother,' he stressed, 'and I want him to go as far as he can in the competition.' But he emphasised that, with both he and his bride working full-time, any spare time would need to be spent making final preparations for the event. Furthermore, he had assured Olly by saying, 'Once the wedding and honeymoon are out of the way, I'll be down there like a shot.'

For now, no more was said about Ben's wedding. But another threat to Olly arrived in early November in the form of a throat infection – the enemy of every singer. Doctors advised him to rest his voice for 48 hours. That meant resting the speaking voice as well as his singing voice. He kept quiet when the finalists turned out for the movie premiere of *A Christmas Carol*, starring Jim Carrey and Colin Firth, in London's Leicester Square. Finally, Olly made a recovery. 'I saw the doctor and had an injection in my bum,' he told the *Sun*. 'Apparently, the antibiotics get into the bloodstream faster that way.'

Only days later, on Tuesday, 10 November (the start of week six on *The X Factor*), came a further setback. While Olly was working out in the house gym, he hit a punch-bag with such force that he cracked one of the bones in his right hand. No one was sure why he had been hitting it quite so hard but, after being given an X-ray check at London's University College Hospital, he would have to wear a cast on his hand for his performance of Queen's 'Don't Stop Me Now' for the next live final, to prevent any further damage. 'He's confident it won't affect his hip-swivelling moves!' promised an *X Factor* spokesperson.

But it was soon announced that striking the punch-bag had aggravated a previous injury from an argument with his brother Ben. 'They were mucking around as brothers do and things got a bit heated,' said a source in the *Sunday Mirror*. 'Olly hit his brother on the head but he was the one who came off worse. Olly never had the injury treated properly, so it's never completely healed.'

The pressure in the spotlight is particularly acute for the solo artist where health is concerned. It's arguably more stressful than for a member of a group. If one member of a group felt under the weather or unwell, the others might be able to cover for them. For a solo act, there was nowhere to hide. You might not have to share the spotlight with others but the focus was all on you. It was no different if you were having an off day.

By the end of November 2009, there were just two weeks to go until *The X Factor*'s grand final. With just five contestants remaining (Lloyd Daniels in what would be his swansong week, Danyl, Stacey, Joe and Olly), from now on each remaining contestant had to perform two songs every Saturday night. At least the judging panel no longer had any power of elimination – in these latter stages, the public had the final say.

Week eight's themes were 'Elton John' and 'Take That'. Olly's remaining rival in the Over-25s category, Danyl, would cover Elton's 'Your Song', which Olly had tentatively covered at bootcamp stage. His Take That choice was 'Relight My Fire', a hit for the group (with Lulu) in 1993 but written and first recorded by Dan Hartman in 1979. Olly also had one ballad and something more uptempo. Against Sir Elton's barnstorming 'Saturday Night's Alright for Fighting', he tackled the Gary Barlow-penned ballad, 'Love Ain't Here Anymore', the only Take That single in three years during the mid-1990s that failed to reach the British number one spot.

Relatives of the contestants were sometimes suspicious that they were being given unsuitable material to perform on the show. Olly's sister Fay, who worked as a veterinary nurse, was not quite convinced that her sibling was being given the best treatment and said in one newspaper of his Over-25s rival, 'Sometimes Danyl gets the better song choices. I hear what they are both singing and I think, "Where is Simon coming from with that?" Olly always delivers. If he was singing a Justin Timberlake track, he'd win hands down.'

Olly's 'Love Ain't Here Anymore' particularly pleased one female audience member. He began his rendition of the song by singing it in front of her, before making his way to the stage. 'You're back in your stride again,' encouraged Cheryl Cole, though Dannii was more critical: 'The sparkle wasn't quite in the eyes.'

Later reflecting on his *X Factor* experiences, Olly revealed how, for a time, he felt in the shadow of a rival Simon protégé. 'Danyl was the one everyone was talking about. He was probably the favourite to win in our group. Not because Simon was treating anyone differently, it was just that he was getting more attention. It was paranoia on my part.' Because Olly sensed that he wasn't getting Simon's full attention (in the earlier stages he seemed more interested in Danyl and Jamie), it made him work harder for approval. 'I always had this edge with Simon. I always felt I had to impress him every time.'

On Monday, 30 November 2009, as everyone began preparing for that Saturday's semi-final, the thorny subject of Ben's wedding came back. On that day, any possibility that Olly could yet attend the ceremony was extinguished once and for all. Simon Cowell felt that, even if Olly took just a few hours off from rehearsals, it could affect the quality of the live transmitted show, especially as it was the series semi-final. Olly expressed great regret. 'I'm gutted – I had no idea when I auditioned in May it would ever come to this. But Ben says he understands and we'll do something after the show is over.'

Others close to the family expressed disappointment more vociferously. Simon would not arrange for a taxi motorbike or helicopter to take Olly on the 30-mile round trip from Wembley to Chelmsford. 'Olly can't believe they couldn't come to some sort of arrangement,' said one friend. 'Ben's only going to get married once and, like any twin brother, Olly had always dreamed of being his best man.'

So Tommy Bradley, the alternative best man, stepped in. A friend of Olly's too, he regretted Olly's absence on Ben's big day. 'Olly is always the life and soul of the party,' he said. 'I'm over the moon that he's in the semi-finals but I am going to miss him on the day. I was hoping for some help with the speech but Olly is a bit busy singing, dancing and rehearsing.'

Another wedding guest was quoted in the press as saying: 'Ben was so happy and Amy looked absolutely stunning. Everyone had a great time – but it was obvious a little something was missing. Olly really should have been there. Everyone was talking about him, how amazing it is that he made it so far on *The X Factor*, but how it was a shame he couldn't be there. No one blames him though. Everyone understands he is pursuing a once-in-a-lifetime shot. Hopefully it will all be worth it in the end.'

Instead, it was announced that Olly planned to congratulate Ben and his bride live on the show. During the afternoon, he was reduced to listening to the wedding on his mobile phone. Ben was not impressed. 'Cowell could have made this happen,' he fumed to the *Sunday Mirror* in an article published the day after his wedding. 'But he refused. I thought he'd have a bit more

Christmas spirit. But he's turned out to be nothing more than Mr Scrooge.' According to Ben, the production team had been approached about the clash weeks before but 'they kept saying, "Wait and see if he gets through." But surely it would have made sense to put a plan in place just in case.'

In missing his twin's big day, Olly Murs had made quite a sacrifice. He knew that to have pulled out of *The X Factor* at this late stage would have almost certainly ended his prospects of stardom. The show had to go on.

CHAPTER EIGHT

THE
HOMECOMING

On Saturday, 5 December 2009, while Ben's wedding day was taking place in Chelmsford, Olly busied himself with last-minute preparations for the *X Factor* semi-final. The week's very special guest would be Janet Jackson, who would offer her verdict on the remaining four contestants' versions of hits by her late brother Michael. The previous day, Olly, Joe, Stacey and Danyl had visited an exhibition of Michael memorabilia at the O2, the same venue at which he had been intending to play 50 concerts before his untimely death.

For the show itself, Joe would deliver the tear-jerking 'She's Out of My Life', Danyl would sing the show-stopping 'The Man in the Mirror', while Stacey would tackle the more uptempo 'The Way You Make Me Feel'. All three had been 1980s solo hits for Jackson, but Olly's song would be one that Michael had sung as part of his family singing group, The Jacksons. 'Can You Feel It?' had been a British top-ten hit in 1981.

Second song choices in the semi-final came from a variety of sources. Stacey took on 'Somewhere' from the musical *West Side Story*, Joe tackled rock group Journey's song, 'Open Arms', while Danyl opted for Whitney Houston's 'I Have Nothing' from *The Bodyguard*. Olly's second song had two reference points to artists he'd covered before. 'We Can Work It Out' was written by the Beatles' John Lennon and Paul McCartney in 1965 and became that year's Christmas number one for the Fab Four as a double-A sided hit with their equally acclaimed 'Day Tripper'. However, Olly's interpretation was based on Stevie Wonder's cover of the song in 1970.

'I like the fact you didn't pick a really well-known song,' said Louis of 'We Can Work It Out', apparently unaware that it was a Beatles classic. Dannii was hopeful that the song 'showed the best side of your vocal ability'. 'I really hope people are gonna pick up the phone,' said Cheryl. Simon, like Louis, also omitted to mention the Lennon/McCartney connection. 'This takes me back to the very first time we saw you because this is a Stevie Wonder song.' Whether it was an accidental or conscious slip, Simon was subtly reminding the viewing public of Olly's extraordinary debut on *The X Factor* back in September, with his fully formed audition cover of Wonder's 'Superstition'. He finished with the same level of unequivocal support he had given Olly throughout the series. 'You thoroughly deserve your place next week in the final.'

THE HOMECOMING

On learning that he had survived yet again, to make it through to the series final, Olly broke down in tears on Simon's shoulder and thanked everyone for their support. But the odds from William Hill for the final showed that Joe remained the favourite to win at 4/11. Stacey and Olly were, respectively, 3/1 and 5/1.

Olly was Simon's last protégé in the contest. Danyl would not be in the final and quashed suggestions that there were strained relations between him and Olly. Indeed, he backed him to win. 'I'm so proud of him – he's a guy that came from nothing and I think that's just a brilliant story. I'm going to see him next week and I'm going to have my "Go Olly" T-shirt and be supporting him.'

The guests were announced for *The X Factor* finals weekend. As well as Sir Paul McCartney performing a solo spot for the Sunday-night climax, three very special guests would duet with the finalists. Michael Bublé would sing with Stacey Solomon, George Michael with Joe McElderry, and Robbie Williams would team up with Olly. With this sort of line-up in prospect, the show's producers hoped it would be the only topic of conversation when everyone went back to work or school on the Monday morning.

What was Olly going to wear? If he had any say in the matter, something like a suit. 'When they give me the tight trousers, it's a bit off,' he said with a sigh to the *Sun*. 'I'd rather people were watching me for my voice and not being distracted by my other attributes.' He revealed another weekly routine, which was not conducted before the cameras – a spray tan, which took place every Friday. 'They give me a top-half one. I'm not going to go full because I'm never going to get my legs out now it's winter.'

And so the last hectic week of the competition was underway. There was hardly time for anyone to catch their breath – immediately after the semi-final, Olly, Joe and Stacey found themselves in Simon's dressing room discussing material for the final weekend. On the Monday, resident singing coach Yvie Burnett spent the day working out how to adapt and edit the performers' song selections. Meanwhile, choreographer Brian Friedman began preparing dance moves and staging, just as stylist Faye Sawyer considered suitable outfits for the singers.

At least there was no longer any room-sharing at the *X Factor* house. Olly, Joe and Stacey each had their own en-suite bedroom. Not that there was much time for relaxation. As part of the build-up to the final, each finalist hoped to drum up some last-minute local support by travelling back to their home town or city with their respective mentor. A rapturous reception would await them all. Unknown to most people only three months earlier, they had put their respective towns on the map.

Joe's hero's welcome came first. He visited South Shields with Cheryl on Monday, 7 December 2009. The following day, Stacey was off to Dagenham with Dannii. There she was reunited with her toddler son, Zach, as well as giving special performances at her old secondary school and a theatre in the town of Barking.

Olly Murs' triumphant homecoming took place on Wednesday, 9 December. The towns of Witham and nearby Colchester were incredibly excited at the prospect of his visit. But it was not his first visit back home. Everyone had been keeping up with his progress for some time.

In mid-November he had made a brief visit to Witham with a film crew to capture some of the reactions of the locals to the town's new star. A return visit to his local pub, The George, caused so much delighted interest that the police had to be called during his two hours there. 'He was like the President, signing autographs and kissing babies,' said the pub landlord, John Fisher who, through karaoke nights and gigs held at his establishment, had known of Olly's star potential before most.

Throughout his days on *The X Factor*, Olly had not forgotten his roots, his friends or his work colleagues. Tony Last, the chairman of Olly's former football team Witham Town FC, confirmed that fame hadn't affected him in a negative way. 'He came up and saw us,' said the chairman. 'He's not too big for that. We asked him how he got on and he said, "You've got to watch it."' Olly's boss in his recruitment days, Robyn Holmes, was thrilled to see him too. 'Everyone is rooting for him,' she said, 'and he has popped into the office, so we know he is really excited. He has sung for us in the past, at Christmas parties, and we always thought what a talented singer he was.'

To some in the town, Olly's abilities as a singer came as

a surprise. Keith Ferguson had taught Olly PE at Notley High School, where the youngster became a star centre-forward in the school football team. 'I was absolutely staggered when I saw him on *The X Factor*,' said the teacher. 'I didn't have a clue he could sing or dance. It's funny because he never used to sing football songs on the way to matches in the school mini-bus.' Though admittedly it's tough to make the average football song or chant sound like blue-eyed soul.

His soccer-playing friends of old praised Olly's realistic attitude to celebrity, despite his very sudden rise out of obscurity. 'It's been fantastic,' said Kirk Setford. 'Olly gets more and more confident but it's confident rather than cocky – he is still massively himself and has not changed one little bit.' Witham Town FC's Matt Dean had been convinced of Olly's fate for some time. 'Knowing him as I do,' he told one reporter, 'I always thought he would have the talent to shock people and go on to win it.'

There were even local businesses which, during November, had taken advantage of having a new local celebrity in their midst. One café, in tribute to Olly's regular custom, had named an all-day breakfast after him to raise money for Children in Need. The clientele of one Witham pub, meanwhile, had toasted the singer with a new limited-edition beer called Olly Olly Olly. It was described to one local newspaper as (deep breath) 'a full-flavoured, thirst-quenching amber-coloured session bitter with a biscuit maltiness, moderate bitterness and citrus hop aroma and finish'.

THE HOMECOMING

By Wednesday, 9 December, Essex couldn't wait to see Olly Murs, who would be accompanied on his flying visit by Simon Cowell. For his first stop, he was flown to Notley High School in Braintree, the secondary school he attended in the second half of the 1990s. To a packed hall of excited youngsters and staff, he performed his now familiar cover of Stevie Wonder's 'Superstition'. Briefly assuming the role of acting head teacher, Simon joked with the pupils that the existing head had made a promise of no homework.

Next, Olly and Simon visited Witham itself. 'Everyone was going crazy as we walked around,' said Olly. 'I kept telling Simon they were screaming for him but he insisted that all the cheering was for me.' During afternoon tea at the Murs family home, Simon was treated to butterscotch Angel Delight. Ever the critic, he suggested that the dessert 'could have done with a little more milk'. It was a surreal experience for the Murs family, especially Olly's parents. 'They were like, "I can't believe Simon Cowell's using our loo!"' said Olly. 'Even though you know it's something everyone does, it still seemed strange because it was him.'

The climax of Olly and Simon's mini-tour of Essex came early on Wednesday evening. It was a mini-Olly gig at a leisure centre in Colchester, complete with a red-carpet welcome. He would take the stage at 7.30 p.m. but fans of all ages began gathering over four hours earlier. The place had never seen scenes like it, as police on horseback had to contain the crowds outside. The chief inspector in charge of the operation admitted that organising police presence was as hard as predicting the scale of the event. 'Anything from six hundred to six thousand people have turned up at similar events,' said Chief Inspector Adrian Coombs. 'We just didn't know how many people would turn up for the event, which was organised at forty-eight-hours notice.'

Long before Olly and Simon arrived in the leisure-centre car park in a black Rolls-Royce, singing, chanting and, of course, screaming filled the air. As the two got out, Olly soaked up the love and euphoria all around, and awarded kisses to mums and their daughters in the crowd, before going inside the building to perform a set.

Olly remained philosophical about his chances of winning the series. 'I'd never say I was the best singer,' he said to one reporter, 'but I would say I was one of the best performers. I know how lucky I am. All I can do is continue working, keep believing in myself and, hopefully, the people at home will do the same.' He told his local paper about his innate motivation: 'It proves that, if you believe in yourself and you go for it, it's not necessarily having someone to push you. I worked my ass off and, not in a cocky way, but I have done this all myself.'

After the Colchester concert, it was back to London. 'I was completely gobsmacked,' said Olly of his visit, seeing the effect of his growing celebrity on the town he knew so well. But he knew his ambition was increasing and to go back to the life he had known would not be enough.

'I have missed my friends and family because I'm a working-class boy. I haven't missed the call centre at all. My old colleagues are great but, if I went back there, it would be a failure.'

Simon Cowell had watched Olly Murs return to his roots and treat his fans with love, respect and humility. Now, as they returned to the capital to continue preparations for the *X Factor* grand final, he reflected on what he had seen in Braintree, Witham and Colchester. 'I got to know him a bit more. I saw what he was like with a crowd. He's like a new Robbie.' And as his street planned a special party to coincide with the Sunday-night final results, it felt like the whole county of Essex was willing him to win.

CHAPTER NINE

A NATIONAL OBSESSION

Simon Cowell knew how hungry Olly Murs was for recognition. He was aware that Olly had worked hard but had overcome setbacks and even experienced a somewhat directionless period in his early to mid-twenties. Before he became one of the richest and most successful entertainment figures in the world, Cowell, too, had his wilderness years. In fact, after spells in a London hi-fi shop and the post room at EMI Records (where his dad, Eric, worked as a director), Simon's early days in the music industry had been ignominious to the point of being risible. One of the first singles he tried to market to the British public was 'Ruff Mix' by Wonderdog in 1982 – a record featuring synthesised dog barks.

By the end of the 1980s, his various record labels had a few hits to their credit – Sinitta's 'So Macho' had nearly been a number one in 1986 – but little in the way of credibility or staying power. But in the early 1990s, he saw that mainstream television could work together with the music industry to create hits. This way of thinking led to a string of novelty hits by TV stars: *Big Breakfast* puppets Zig and Zag, the Mighty Morphin Power Rangers and the World Wrestling Federation Allstars.

The music industry only really started to take Simon Cowell seriously, though, in the spring of 1995. He approached Robson Green and Jerome Flynn, cast members of the ITV drama *Soldier, Soldier*, to ask if they would re-record a cover version of 'Unchained Melody' they had sung in an episode of the long-running series. Neither was particularly keen to record it at first but, after careful persuasion, caved in to Cowell's request. It would top the UK charts for seven weeks, sell well over a million copies and become the biggest-selling single of the year. Other Robson and Jerome singles – all covers – would top the charts. Meanwhile, Cowell bankrolled more TV tie-ins: cast members of *Heartbeat*, *Coronation Street*, *Emmerdale* and *Gladiators*. Then, in 1997, came the million-selling 'Teletubbies Say "Eh-oh!"'

Even after he had launched boy band Five and helped Louis Walsh to unveil Westlife in 1999, Cowell arguably understood TV values better than those of music. Over a decade later, by which time the world knew Cowell for *American Idol*, *Britain's Got Talent* and *The X Factor*, *The Times*'s writer Will Hodgkinson summed up the appeal of *The X Factor* as 'never about singing, but soap opera'. He went on to explain, 'The audience would share the tears and joys of the show's heroes and villains, its rank outsiders and its firm favourites. Then, when a tiny handful of contestants go on to have successful pop careers, a record-buying audience already feels that they know them.'

The rock press, needless to say, loathed everything Cowell represented. The music he pushed had little or no credibility. More surprisingly, other purveyors of teenybop pop were suspicious of his vehicles. Pete Waterman, one third of Stock Aitken Waterman, whose discoveries had included Kylie Minogue, Jason Donovan and Steps, knew a thing or two about manufactured pop. He had even worked alongside Cowell on the panels of *Pop Idol* and *Popstars: The Rivals*, the series that discovered Will Young and Girls Aloud (featuring, of course, Cheryl Cole).

But Waterman felt uneasy about *The X Factor* and argued that the format lacked distinctive personalities. 'If you're a good singer with a happy home life, you won't get past the first audition,' he told the *Independent on Sunday*. 'If you've got one leg, an ailing spouse and are living on a sink estate, you've hit the jackpot.' Waterman's view was obviously an exaggeration but he wasn't alone in his view. 'It has put music back decades,' said Sting, who as ex-lead singer of The Police, had his own period as a pin-up and pop idol. 'It is a soap opera which has nothing to do with music. They are either Mariah Carey or Whitney Houston or Boyzone and are not encouraged to create a unique signature. That cannot come from TV.'

Other pop icons wondered how musical innovation could emerge from the production line of the show. Sir

Elton John dismissed the whole enterprise as a 'cruise-ship show'. 'Some great talent has come from that,' said Moby. 'But the musicians I love are the ones who write their own songs. You [know] that they wrote it and they cared about it.' Noddy Holder, ex-lead singer of Slade, said of the show, 'The chase for fame overshadows the thirst for music... There's no experimentation at all. They're not moving forward and they're not giving off-the-wall acts the chance.'

Slade's 'Merry Xmas Everybody' from 1973 was, perhaps, the definitive British Christmas number one but, since 2004, the top of the Yuletide charts had been dominated by *The X Factor*'s winning songs. As each series drew to a close in mid-December, the contest winner would have a single released within hours of their triumph. They were almost guaranteed a number one in Christmas week. But the winner of *The X Factor* 2009 would have an unseasonal foil. It would be an anti-*X Factor* protest vote and it came from an unlikely source.

'Killing in the Name' by Rage Against the Machine had been a hit once before, reaching the top 30 in Britain early in 1993. Politically and environmentally aware, the American rock band were an antidote to the sort of glossy pop that existed long before *The X Factor* was invented. 'Killing in the Name' was angry, noisy and 'sweary' but, thanks to a well-organised Internet campaign and during an era when any downloaded song was eligible for the charts, it looked like challenging *The X Factor*'s monopoly of the Christmas number-one spot.

As it turned out, Rage Against the Machine's back catalogue was owned by Sony Music anyway, the same corporation that distributed Syco's products. But Simon Cowell felt that, if this was a campaign, even a campaign aimed at him, it was a 'stupid' one and would most likely spoil the finalists' festive season: 'Me having a number one at Christmas is not going to change my life particularly. It does, however, change these guys' lives. It's quite a cynical campaign geared at me, which is going to spoil the party for these three.'

He also felt the campaign was 'dismissive of the people who watch and enjoy the show, to treat our audiences as if they're stupid, and I don't like that.'

BBC Radio 1 DJ Edith Bowman wondered if reality-TV vehicles like *The X Factor* distorted the process of celebrity, encouraging fame rather than talent. She thought back to her own pop idols as having 'an element of mystique about them and they had some incredible talent. That's not what celebrity is about anymore.' She shared the concerns of many that the hunger for fame was a quick fix, especially for young people. But she argued that society in general had a responsibility in how it discussed celebrity. Some could be forgiven for thinking that fame is the benchmark of achievement.

Simon Cowell denied that *The X Factor* was a quick passport to fame or a pop lottery. 'I'm not responsible for people expecting instant gratification in life,' he told the *Daily Mirror*. 'Because of the way *X Factor* works, normally the people who get voted for are the ones who've worked hard. What we talk about constantly is that hard work is the thing that's going to get you what you want.' It was a belief shared by Olly Murs. He was under no illusion that working in the entertainment business was anything other than gruelling. Enjoyable, sure, but extremely hard work.

Even if you worked hard, you wouldn't be guaranteed a positive write-up. In early December 2009, before *The X Factor*'s final had even taken place, Olly was one act who was in the press's firing line. One writer in the *Daily Telegraph* summed up his image as 'Will Young crossed with Fireman Sam'. He went on to predict that, based on Murs' long-term musical prospects, he 'might as well start packing for the next series of *I'm a Celebrity*'. At the time of writing, nearly three years and a few million record sales later, Olly Murs still has no plans to enter the jungle.

With a General Election looming in the spring of 2010, some political commentators considered why so many young adults were so keen to pick up the phone to vote for an *X Factor* contestant but less enthusiastic when it came to visiting the ballot box. The *Sun* newspaper would wonder why, 'while millions of young people will vote on *X Factor*, they are less keen to choose a Government'. Although around 60 per cent of the 44 million-strong electorate had turned out for the 2005 General Election, on that occasion, just 37 per cent of the 18–24 age group bothered to vote. Interestingly, while they were about it, the paper checked the voting habits of the three *X Factor* finalists' constituencies. Joe's South Shields had a 50 per cent turnout, with Stacey's locale of Dagenham just ahead on 51 per cent. But it was Olly's Witham that was far ahead, with 65 per cent of the eligible electorate voting, higher than the national average.

Olly himself, though, fared less well in a YouGov poll commissioned by the *Sun*, who approached over 2,000 regular viewers of *The X Factor* (aged 18 and over) and asked which of the three finalists they would vote for. With the younger demographic (18–34-year-olds), he had the highest share of the vote – some 32 per cent – 2 points in front of favourite Joe and some way ahead of Stacey (who attracted just 18 per cent). But it was a completely different story with the over-55s category, an age group which enjoyed *The X Factor*, too. Joe was the overwhelming winner there, with 52 per cent of the vote, against only 15 per cent for Stacey and a paltry 11 per cent for Olly. Overall, the poll revealed that only 20 per cent would vote for Olly to win the final, a better result than for Stacey (17 per cent). But Joe's share was an impressive 43 per cent.

Though Olly's belief that he was technically not as good a singer as Joe was born out by the same poll (only 10 per cent against Joe's 68 per cent), he scored much more highly in the best dancer (a commanding 71 per cent) and – perhaps a hint at his popularity to come – was voted the finalist that most fans wanted to take down the pub for a pint. He knew that Joe's voice would move someone, whereas his voice was more likely to make people want to get up and dance.

Perhaps mindful of the impending General Election, in

which it was vital to capture the youth vote, several political figures offered their support to Joe McElderry. David Miliband, the MP for Joe's constituency in South Shields, wrote to the teenager to wish him good luck. Ben Bradshaw, the Culture Secretary at the time, turned up at *The X Factor*'s studios to pass on his best wishes. Even the then-Prime Minister Gordon Brown (visiting Afghanistan) sent a message of good luck.

As the political elite gave the thumbs-up to the show, millions continued to watch and the mainstream media endorsed its values. But its format was by no means popular with everyone. Some believed that there was a surfeit of pop smeared with Simon Cowell's fingerprints. Niggling doubts lingered about whether *The X Factor* was sufficiently interested in distinctively British music, the sort of attitude which had produced giants over the years like The Kinks, Madness, The Smiths, Kate Bush, Pet Shop Boys, Oasis and Pulp.

Daily Mail columnist Paul Connolly felt that Cowell's series marked a 'betrayal of our pop culture. One had only to watch the American singing voices adopted by both Joe McElderry and Olly Murs to realise that Cowell feels not a jot of pride that his home country has produced bands and acts as magical and exciting as The Beatles, Dusty Springfield, Blur and Radiohead.' Instead, Connolly wrote, Leona Lewis, Alexandra Burke and others were aping the styles of 'American caterwaulers' like Mariah and Whitney, 'singers who mistake multi-octave showiness for emotion'.

A NATIONAL OBSESSION

Entering *The X Factor* was a decision not to be taken lightly. As the *Sun* would reveal in June 2011 (in a story headlined PUT THE SI INTO SILENCE), those auditioning would find they were entering into a professional relationship with the programme. Taking to the stage in the live auditions, each hopeful would be handed a four-page contract with some strict rules. Once that contract was signed, the contestant would be forbidden from talking about the judges publicly, or even allowed to discuss the hosts like Dermot O'Leary. Prohibited from 'tweeting' or posting Facebook messages about any of the above, they could not share pictures of their experiences on the show with their friends. Another clause dictated that the wannabes would have to seek 'prior written consent of a senior executive of the Company' to talk about them. Essentially, as a component of *The X Factor* machine, they were bound by a set of rules and regulations that anyone starting a job would be faced with.

Were Simon Cowell and his label, Syco Records, the real winners of every year's *X Factor* series? Media public-relations expert Mark Borkowski was in little doubt. Speaking in late 2009, he said, 'While the winner is likely to go straight into the one-hit wonder category, the show goes on and on. For a reality show to have this much hype and interest, and such huge audiences after six series is quite extraordinary.' For Peter Fincham, the head of ITV, Cowell's creations like *The X Factor* and *Britain's Got Talent* helped define British television in the 21st century. 'They have become more than just a talking point,' said Fincham. 'They are a national obsession.' And it seemed as if the whole country was talking about Olly, Joe and Stacey.

CHAPTER TEN

FINAL AND AFTERMATH

The winning song for *The X Factor* 2009 might have been Journey's 'Don't Stop Believin'', a song Joe McElderry had already performed in Rock Week. Then there was a change of plan. Simon Cowell's alternative was to be 'The Climb', originally sung by US teenage star Miley Cyrus. Considered an ideal choice for Stacey Solomon, legal issues still needed to be ironed out with Columbia Records, who owned the rights to the song.

'The Climb', taken from the Disney-made movie spin-off of the Cyrus TV series *Hannah Montana*, is a power ballad about challenges, about following dreams, with lots of imagery about scaling mountains and fighting battles. About what's waiting on the other side. It's about striving for success and persevering, and about facing doubts head-on. As with so many songs chosen for *The X Factor*, its lyrics talked of effort in order to achieve.

From early December, all the remaining finalists began rehearsing the song, each wondering if their version would be the one available to buy within hours of their winning the competition. The finalists would all have a promotional video shot for their recorded version, to be based on a Chanel perfume commercial which had starred Nicole Kidman. But while Kidman had been standing atop skyscrapers in New York, the *X Factor* hopefuls would be seen dancing in puddles against the skyline of London. Only the winner's recording and video of 'The Climb' would be made public.

On Thursday, 10 December, the last three *X Factor* finalists talked to the press. Joe, Stacey and Olly had all been warned by Cowell that 'winning is more important than ever before'. The rivalry between them was healthy though. 'There is going to be competitiveness because we all want to win,' said Olly, 'but I think the only competition is yourself. I've got to make sure I go out and do the best performance I can. If it's not good enough, I know in my heart it's my time to go.'

Olly wasn't really convinced he was going to win but he was not downhearted. Asked what he might do if he lost in the final, Olly had a tongue-in-cheek answer ready. Maybe he'd set up a market stall selling hats, or even sneak some Murs merchandise into the shops, like calendars. 'Apparently all the girls like me, so I'll be able to get my flat pack out,' he joked.

He had done well regardless. When asked which of the three had made the biggest improvement over the past few months, vocal coach Yvie Burnett insisted all had made excellent progress but specifically said of Olly that 'he's done incredibly well with his ballads. He wasn't so confident when he started.'

Olly was picking up some celebrity fans too. He revealed in the *Sunday Mirror* that he had the support of two warring siblings – Liam and Noel Gallagher, by now estranged after one row too many in their group Oasis. 'Liam got in touch to say he was a fan and that he liked my style,' said Olly. 'He sent loads of clothes from his new fashion range for me to wear on the show.' Before long, Noel had contacted him too by text 'to say he was a fan too and that he liked my voice. I'm a massive Oasis fan. I'd love to get them back together.'

The late Amy Winehouse was also said to have made her feelings known towards Olly. They encountered each other at a nightclub where he had gone to watch a set by Hackney-born rapper Professor Green. Amy urgently shouted out to Olly to try and engage him conversation. 'He looked a little scared,' said a witness, 'but, before he had a chance to do anything, she grabbed his arm and took him off for a chat.'

On the Friday, the judges took their places to watch the performances take shape, while the show's technicians worked out sound levels and camera angles, aiming (as usual) to create a flawless piece of live television entertainment that was both slick and exciting. *The X Factor*, even in its sixth year, remained one of ITV's most popular programmes and it was estimated that 20 million people would tune in for the climactic stages of the series, with advertising slots said to be available for £400,000 per minute. In addition, Cowell was about to take the format of the show to America, where the Fox TV network would begin transmitting it from 2011.

On Saturday, 12 December 2009, *The X Factor* finals weekend finally arrived. Prince Harry and his partner Chelsy Davy sat in the studio audience in Wembley. On a live link, down in Colchester, over a thousand fans were crammed into the Ivor Crewe Lecture Theatre at Essex University.

Each of the three remaining finalists had to sing two songs solo, plus take part in a duet with a very famous artist. Olly duetted with Robbie Williams on Williams' 1997 hit 'Angels'. After singing the first section of the song alone, Olly introduced his duettist with the words, 'I can't believe I'm saying this... !' Due to a misunderstanding over his opening cue, a nervous Robbie fluffed his first line. He was bowled over by Olly's performance and by how calmly he had dealt with the confusion. 'I can't believe how confident this man is,' he said of Olly and quipped, 'I should be taking tips from him!' Afterwards, the ex-Take That star reflected, 'It's a weird show to be on because *X Factor* is based around judgement. But if you're not judging yourself too well, it's a show that can get to you. I think that's why so many people threw a wobbler up there, because they know they're being judged.

After their duet, Robbie would keep in touch with

Olly. He invited him to play football in his garden at his Los Angeles home.

For his solo-song choices, Olly revived two of his earlier party pieces: 'Superstition' from the audition and, from week two of the live finals, 'A Fool in Love'. Having originally criticised the choice of 'A Fool in Love', Louis had clearly changed his mind by finals weekend. 'That was my favourite song of yours of the whole series,' he told Olly. 'You owned the stage, you owned the song.' Cheryl said, 'You thoroughly deserve your place in the final.' Eventually, Simon Cowell, Olly's mentor, spoke. 'I've got to know you well. I've got to know your family. You've been an absolute pleasure to work with. I am so proud of you, Olly. I'm really happy I chose you to be in my top twelve.'

Stacey was gone after the Saturday show. Then there were two. Joe and Olly. But there were signs that, whether Olly triumphed or fell at the final hurdle, his mentor might stick around after all. 'I think this guy, looked after properly and given some decent records, could do really, really well,' Simon Cowell told the press in articles published on the day of the final. Former contestants were canvassed for their views on those still in the running. Edward Grimes of Jedward paid tribute to Olly's dancing and said what might propel him into a rosy pop future was humour and charm. 'If he uses his charm with the ladies, he can definitely still win. A lot of ladies like him and, if he uses that in his performance, he'll get more votes.'

'The Climb' may have been a song for a singer like Joe McElderry rather than an entertainer like Olly Murs. Regardless, on the last Sunday night of the series − 13 December − Olly gave the song his all. 'You absolutely tore it from your soul,' gasped Cheryl Cole. Louis Walsh called him 'an amazing contestant'. An astonished Dannii Minogue wondered aloud, 'Where did that come from? You held it together. A voice we've never heard before.' 'You just answered every criticism that you're not a very good singer' began Simon Cowell. 'I can see how much this means to you. I really, really hope everyone gets behind you after that performance.'

Many people did get behind Olly. But not enough to triumph. That Sunday night, Joe McElderry won *The X Factor* 2009, in front of a studio audience that included the likes of Katie Price and Ronan Keating. He had secured 61 per cent of the public vote. His prize was a recording contract worth £1 million and it began with the immediate release of 'The Climb' as a single.

Joe plugged the single with many high-profile appearances, including the *Sun*'s Military Awards ('The Millies') held at the Imperial War Museum in South London. It was rumoured that Cowell was lining him up as a new Zac Efron and taking him to Hollywood. Before any of that happened, though, there was a whistle-stop tour of TV spots and interviews on Joe's first Monday morning as *X Factor* champ. Then it was off to the BBC for the recording of the annual edition of *Top of the Pops*, scheduled to air on Christmas Day.

Unfortunately for Joe and Syco Records, 'The Climb' was not number one for Christmas. The Rage Against the Machine Internet campaign had been successful and 'Killing in the Name' became the biggest seller for the festive season, although Joe's single would belatedly climb to the top on 27 December, vindication not only for Joe himself, but for the judge who had been backing him throughout the whole series, namely his mentor Cheryl Cole.

Meanwhile, controversy over the choice of song for the winner continued to bubble. Cowell denied that 'The Climb' suited Joe's style far more than the other competitors. 'When we record the song, we try it out with the last five contestants and, if anyone can't sing the song, we [won't] do it.' He maintained that Olly's version was every bit as good as Joe's and insisted, 'Olly really liked the song and was comfortable with it.'

Olly was proud of his achievement in coming second but was gracious in defeat. 'Joe has been phenomenal every single week,' he said. Louis Walsh would subsequently stress, 'Olly, you didn't lose, you were in the final. You got a record deal. And as long as you work and get good songs, that's it.' Simon Cowell agreed with his fellow judge: 'He didn't walk away a loser. It always felt like he'd work in the real world.' But in December 2009, Olly Murs' survival in pop was by no means guaranteed. He had done his utmost but, nonetheless, had lost out to Joe McElderry. 'I'm not gonna lie and say he wasn't gutted, because he was gutted,' said Simon Cowell later.

'When you've lost, words don't mean an awful lot. You've got to work it out yourself.'

It got worse. As Olly left the *X Factor* house in Golders Green for the final time and was consoled outside by his mum Vicky-Lynn, voting figures for the series revealed that he had not been first in the weekly public vote on a single occasion across the series. In fact, had the judges left the decision to the viewing public in week seven, it would not have been Jedward who would have been shown the door. It would have been Olly Murs.

But maybe winning wasn't everything. Coming second or third did not necessarily harm a future career. In its first series in 2004, the runners-up were vocal quartet G4, who wowed everyone with their unique interpretation of Queen's 'Bohemian Rhapsody'. They would last longer in the charts than winner Steve Brookstein. Ray Quinn (who lost out to Leona Lewis in 2006) would later win *Dancing on Ice* on ITV and went on to specialise in musical theatre and pantomimes, while Rhydian Roberts (second in 2007) would appear in *War of the Worlds* with Atomic Kitten member Liz McClarnon.

Male vocal quartet JLS, placed second in 2008, would enjoy considerable success after *The X Factor*. At the end of October 2009, they made a return visit to the *X Factor* fold, this time not as contestants but as hugely successful guest artists, performing their current single, 'Everybody in Love'. Backstage, they offered Olly Murs some invaluable encouragement. Olly had said to them in wonder, 'I am so envious of you guys. You are living the dream.' JLS member Aston Merrygold reassured him, 'Don't worry – you'll be doing this when you leave *The X Factor.*'

Olly stood a good chance of landing his own record deal in 2010, even if he would have to wait until after the release of Joe McElderry's debut album. 'I want to get an album out and a single – that's all I have ever wanted,' said Olly. 'I think I'm quite versatile. I would like to be very much like a Robbie Williams and rock it out like that, or be like Justin Timberlake, dancing and performing.'

But he knew one thing: he did not want his old job back at the call centre in Witham. 'I'm not a doctor or solicitor,' he pointed out. 'I haven't got another career I'm happy about. The only thing that I have ever wanted to get into is singing.' He knew that the months ahead were crucial, laying the groundwork for what he hoped would be a long-term solo career. He feared that he would be a flash in the pan and constantly remembered the lyrics of JLS's song 'One Shot', which urged people to make the most of every chance as you might not get a second one. He felt he had to give it everything he had and try his best.

The months following *The X Factor* final are testing ones for any finalist. The TV exposure is over but the participants may not want the 'dream' to end. While Joe was paraded around TV chat shows in the pre-Christmas rush, Olly and third-placed Stacey were at Gatwick Airport, helping to promote a new karaoke competition for wannabe singers waiting for their flights. At least Olly's

Christmas would be quiet and low key, though. 'It will be good just to sit down. I'm looking forward to my mum's Christmas dinner. And my dad does a wicked cheese sauce for the cauliflower.'

Olly's 2010 would begin in rowdy fashion. A New Year gig on London's Albert Embankment would descend 'into a brawl' in the crowd after three songs. Thereafter he faced a January that was every bit as busy as his previous few months. The only difference was that, for the most part, no cameras were pointing at him. He presided over auditions to find talent for holiday parks across Britain. He provided pre-match or interval entertainment at football and rugby grounds around the country. At one Scottish soccer game, crowds began chanting 'Are you SuBo in disguise?' (in reference to *Britain's Got Talent*'s Susan Boyle) and 'There's only one Joe McElderry'.

Sometimes, as a budding performer, you needed a thick skin to appear at these events. A combination of self-awareness, a good sense of humour and a lot of confidence went a long way. But then, Olly would have been used to spectators chanting – it went all the way back to his days as a semi-pro football player in Witham. He knew how to adapt and how to please the crowd. 'I never really get nervous when I'm singing,' he said. 'For me, it's just a job that I just really love doing. If you can't go out and put on a performance in front of thousands of people, it's not the career for you.'

At this stage, Olly's gigs consisted entirely of covers. They tended to comprise three of his show-stopping numbers from *The X Factor*: Ike and Tina Turner's 'A Fool in Love', The Jacksons' 'Can You Feel It?' and, of course, Stevie Wonder's 'Superstition'. But what may have worked in the context of a hi-tech television extravaganza did not quite have the same level of excitement, somehow, once the results had happened and the competition was over. Reviews of his 20-minute set could be scathing. 'He moonwalked around like an embarrassing uncle let loose on the dance floor,' said one critic of an appearance in the Scottish town of Falkirk, although he conceded that Olly was certainly capable of personalising his performance – changing the lyrics of 'I Wanna Be Like You' from *The Jungle Book* to 'I wanna be Scottish like you', to the delight of the audience. But it didn't seem to be enough. 'Murs looked like a guy who is having a lot of fun being famous,' said the critic with a sigh. 'Sadly, he doesn't look anything like a superstar in waiting.'

Undeterred, Olly was in no doubt about his ambitions for the New Year. They were to follow the example of JLS and return to the show that made his name. In the meantime, the bookings continued. There was the launch of the International Boat Show in London (reuniting him with Stacey Solomon), the engagement bash for the model Danielle Lloyd, a gig for under-18s in Peterborough and one for schoolchildren in the Somerset town of Yeovil. At the end of January, he returned to Essex for two gigs: one in Chelmsford, another in Braintree.

If some of these commitments look modest, even desperate, compared with prime-time TV spots or arena tours, Olly gamely regarded it as work. His philosophy was cheerfully realistic – at least if he didn't succeed in long-term pop stardom, he would have tried his best, and amassed some money. 'I made a deal with myself that I would sing everywhere,' he recalled later. 'I would go to every corner of the country and earn as much as I could. That way I might be able to get a house and maybe even put some money in the bank, and then I would go home and get back to normal life.'

He knew that to be available was half the battle in show business. 'You've just got to work hard. Don't take holidays or say you don't want to do a certain gig. Earn as much money as you can.'

His caution was sensible. For the time being, at least, his superstar friend Robbie Williams wasn't calling. 'His phone must be dead or something. And it does cost a lot to text from LA so maybe he hasn't got the money to spend,' Olly said. Nor was Simon Cowell returning his calls. 'It would be really good to chat to him,' Olly told the *Sun*, 'but I know the judges are all having time off at the moment.' At this rate, would Olly Murs' solo career ever get underway?

CHAPTER ELEVEN

SYCOVILLE

In early February 2010, the call finally came. Olly was set to sign a joint deal with Simon Cowell's Syco Music label and Epic Records, home to JLS. Representatives from the two labels (both part of the mighty Sony Music corporation) were in no doubt that Olly was a key signing, with the sort of talent and longevity to succeed as a pop star. 'As an artist he ticks every box,' agreed Syco's managing director Sonny Takhar. Nick Raphael, the head of Epic, described him as 'a big personality' with 'obvious talents'. In a 2010 TV documentary called *Olly Murs Revealed*, Raphael would point out that immediate, effortless charisma in an artist, which went beyond admiration, was a rare quality and something record executives like him were always looking for. 'If you meet him, if you see him, you like him. And it's very hard for us to find artists who people like.'

As someone who spotted Olly's potential early on, Simon Cowell knew that not only had *The X Factor* helped him to get a foothold in the music industry, Olly had also been an asset to his show. 'He's everything you want in one of these shows. He's talented, hasn't had a break, wasn't going to get a break and has used his time here to his advantage. And most importantly, he loved every second of it.'

The progress of Olly's career still seemed hardly real life, more like a dream. 'If you'd said to me a year ago that I'd be releasing a single and making an album and performing all over the country, I'd have laughed and said, "Yeah, whatever."' He knew exactly who to thank for these opportunities existing for him. 'I don't want to sound cheesy but I have to thank all the people who voted for me on the show, as it's them that kept me in it and allowed me to do this.'

Work would begin on a debut album in April but, before that, there was still some unfinished business with *The X Factor*. In February and March 2010, Olly joined the series' other top 7 finalists for a 54-date arena tour of Britain – the most extensive series tour to date. At some venues, there were two performances per day. They would perform a mix of classic covers, favourites from the series and a special rendition of the charity single, 'You Are Not Alone'. As well as Stacey, Joe and Olly, the cast would comprise Jamie 'Afro' Archer, Lloyd Daniels, Danyl Johnson, Lucie Jones and Jedward.

The tour's itinerary would include Birmingham,

Belfast, Newcastle and London, among many other cities. The *Sun*'s showbiz reporter Gordon Smart attended the first night of the tour at the Echo Arena in Liverpool on 15 February. The show began with the full cast performing the Black Eyed Peas' 'I Gotta Feeling'. For 'Ghostbusters', Jedward were suspended on wires. Olly delighted the audience with 'Twist and Shout' and 'Superstition', and performed an Austin Powers-style routine, backed by female dancers in polka-dot skirts. To complete the night, headlining act Joe sang his number one hit 'The Climb', to be followed by covers of Taylor Swift's 'Love Story' and Elton John's 'Sorry Seems to Be the Hardest Word'.

Some in the press box were left unmoved by Olly's act. 'Just plain hammy without any mitigating gimmicks,' complained *The Scotsman*'s critic of the Glasgow date. A correspondent from another Scottish paper, the *Sunday Mail*, was more satisfied. 'Murs stole the show – for the first 90 minutes, at least. For the final 30 minutes, it was all about Joe.' The writer noted the adulation towards Olly and his moves on stage, but had to confess that the biggest cheers of the whole evening were reserved for Jedward.

As a measure of how Jedward had captured the imagination of the public as the act many loved to hate, they had been awarded three songs, as opposed to the two reserved for most of the other acts. Unlike every other act, aside from winner Joe, they had the advantage of a single to coincide with the tour. It was called 'Under Pressure', based on something between the Queen and

David Bowie hit of the same name from 1981, and Vanilla Ice's 'Ice Ice Baby' in 1990. The single had entered the charts at number two but the novelty quickly wore off and it plummeted to number 12. It seemed the writing was on the wall for John and Edward Grimes. 'We tried our best to make the lads credible recording artists,' a spokesperson for their label, Sony, said. 'But punters just weren't that bothered.'

Jedward were a spectacle but it was hard to appreciate that visual appeal just by hearing their record. Perhaps a live tour (as the *X Factor* jaunt was demonstrating) was a way of developing the Jedward brand. With record companies feeling the bite of the tough economic climate, decisions had to be made about underperforming artists. But the Sony spokesperson predicted that Jedward could 'make a buck touring as a novelty act'. In fact, the twins were swiftly given a second chance – within 48 hours of being dropped by Sony, they were signed to rival label Universal.

By the end of the tour in early April, some newspaper critics had been impressed. Tim de Lisle, a former *Smash Hits* writer, did not have high hopes for the show but was pleasantly surprised. 'Like a teacher directing a school musical,' he wrote in the *Mail on Sunday*, 'somebody had put together a show that played to the singers' strengths: energy, enthusiasm and expressiveness.' If the whole show was a register of cover versions, at least Olly, 'older than the others and more professional', presented his short set 'with practised ease'.

'It just goes on a completely different level,' Olly later said of the *X Factor* tour. 'You don't realise, when you're on *The X Factor*, how big the show is. You don't realise how much it changes your life until you've finished the show.' In the live arenas, with the competition over, the audience had paid to come and see the contestants, a different proposition from watching them from the living room at home and voting by phone.

It was estimated that each of the performers could earn as much as £100,000 each from the tour. Olly was salivating at the prospect of having some income. Looking to the future, he made plans for his grandmother to visit Elvis Presley's Graceland home in the American city of Memphis and intended to buy a property of his own, either in Essex or in central London. 'I still live with my mum and dad, which isn't exactly cool at the age of twenty-five,' he said. Rounding off his shopping list was a new car to replace his Fiat Cinquecento. 'It's not exactly good for picking up the ladies. So I'll definitely be buying a bigger car.' Finally, he would buy a red Fiat 500, which he christened 'Pat'. He loved driving around – it was a rare way of remaining anonymous. Behind the wheel, no one recognised him or wanted a photograph.

After the tour, the eight acts had gone their separate ways. Their *X Factor* experience was over and now they were all on their own. In June 2010, winner Joe McElderry reported that, even though the contest had finished months ago, many of his fans weren't going to forget it. 'Sometimes I forget I actually won *The X Factor*, then I'll be walking down the street and all these girls will come running up to me. I'm still getting used to that.' He pointed out he was not rolling in money. Though his recording contract was worth £1 million, it wasn't quite the windfall it seemed – after studio time and promotional costs were deducted, Joe was left with around £150,000. He accepted that fame could fade at any time but remained upbeat about his fate: 'I've just won the biggest show in Britain. I'm never going to take it for granted but what's the point worrying if I'm going to be a flop? There's nothing I can do about it. I'm not going to live in fear. All I can do is work my hardest.'

Joe set off for Los Angeles to record his debut album, ready for an October release. He was keeping an open mind about future plans, preparing 'some tracks that people won't expect. I like to do different things.'

There were those who doubted Joe's staying power, however. Showbiz gossip sages scratched their heads at the lack of stories about him. He was not a habitual partygoer, nor were there reports of romantic dalliances surfacing. His label Syco, though, was carefully considering the best way to manage the next step of his career. There seemed little point in rushing the recording of his album. It was better to take the time to choose the right material for Joe as carefully as possible.

When Joe announced he was gay in the summer of 2010, Olly Murs was steadfastly supportive towards him. 'I told him nothing was going to change,' he said and continued, 'I know it was a massive thing to do and a lot of people want to delve into his private life. Some guys can be really funny about it and I wanted to tell him he could speak to me as normal. It wasn't just like telling his friends and family – he was telling it to the whole country.'

Meanwhile, Stacey Solomon, placed third on *The X Factor* 2009, still had no record deal and was even cloudier about her music plans. Meetings were taking place but little else seemed to be going on. 'I suppose if the deal doesn't happen, I could go and make the record myself,' she said but was candid about how little she knew about the recording process. 'I have no clue about any of that side and how it works.'

All the same, she was ambitious about what she wanted to achieve on record, suggesting jazz and indie as two areas she wished to cover. 'I don't want to limit myself to one genre,' she announced and it seemed that, even if her music career stalled, she had other ideas: 'It is far from the only thing I want to do. I'd love to get involved... in theatre. If you love singing and it's your passion, of course you want to do theatre. West End stuff would be amazing.'

Prophetically, as it turned out, she also muttered that TV presenting might be an option.

As he prepared to start working on his debut album in April 2010, Olly Murs continued to honour live appearances. It became clear that he was becoming a major draw. Wearing his now-trademark trilby hat and skinny jeans, he played two free concerts at a shopping centre in East Kilbride, Scotland. Four thousand fans turned out to scream their love for him.

It was the start of a summer filled with live commitments for Olly. Lined up were guest spots at racecourses, a Michael Jackson tribute concert in Blackpool and various festivals around the country. At some dates, he was on bills with the likes of Westlife, The Saturdays and Scouting for Girls. Elsewhere, he found himself alongside other runners-up from TV talent shows, some of whom were finding the going tough. But he was determined to get any job done. He loved performing live most of all – wherever the venue might be. 'It doesn't matter if I'm in a pub, club or an arena,' he said. 'I'm always having fun when I'm on stage and I try and get that over to the audience. I love being up there and especially the dancing element to what I do.' Live shows allowed him to be a bit more daring than on pre-watershed TV. 'I can get away with a few things I wouldn't do on live telly, especially for the ladies, if you know what I mean!'

And meanwhile, there was an album to make.

CHAPTER TWELVE

HEY MR
SONGWRITER

Recording an album was a dream come true for Olly Murs – a project he'd been awaiting for so long. But this would be no time for complacency – in fact, the pressure was even more pronounced. 'Expectations are high and you'll have to learn on the job,' he was warned by the boss of his record company. Epic Records' Nick Raphael explained the sheer cost and commitment a record company had to make to an artist. 'To launch an album in the current market, it costs a million pounds – a pretty significant commitment from a record company.' Fortunately, Raphael was convinced that £1 million would be money well spent on Olly Murs. Equally fortunately, Olly seemed to thrive on challenges like this one. 'They wouldn't be investing that kind of money if they didn't believe in me. It's gonna be a bit of pressure but it's pressure that I love and pressure that I want.'

Like many *X Factor* contestants since 2006, Olly had become a client of Modest! – an artist management company founded by Richard Griffiths and Harry Magee. Griffiths and Magee had guided the careers of Leona Lewis, Alexandra Burke, JLS and others to long-term international success. As of 2012, nearly a decade after it was formed, Modest! still represented many of the most popular *X Factor* contestants, including JLS, Leona Lewis, One Direction and the 2011 series winners, Little Mix. It was also steering the careers of *Britain's Got Talent* winner Paul Potts and even the brilliant Basildon-born singer Alison Moyet, 30 years after she had made a striking debut as one half of the duo Yazoo.

Richard Griffiths, one of Modest!'s co-founders, began as an international booking agent for the Australian heavy-rock band AC/DC in the 1970s, before becoming a head of A&R (Artists and Repertoire), a job that involved overseeing the seeking out of music talent. The A&R department of a record company exists to unearth the stars of tomorrow by listening to demo recordings and attending live gigs by artists. In the 1980s, Griffiths had worked in music publishing at Virgin and launched 10 Records, home to artists like Soul II Soul. As the 1990s dawned, he relocated to the USA where, at Sony Music, he nurtured rock acts like Rage Against the Machine and Pearl Jam. Back in the UK in 1998, he joined forces with Simon Cowell and Louis Walsh to sign Westlife to the BMG label. Then in 2000, he made the deal with Cowell which would bring about the creation of Syco Music and

Television. In other words, the mighty world of *The X Factor*, where pop and TV would co-exist.

Griffiths's business partner Harry Magee also had a long and illustrious career in the music industry. He had worked in record company marketing, before heading Big Life Records and, from 1994, A&M Records. Along the way, he had dealt with artists ranging from Lisa Stansfield, Sting and Bryan Adams to Sheryl Crow and Whitney Houston. As Managing Director at BMG's RCA label from 1998, he, too, was involved in the signing of the group Westlife. From 2001, Harry and Richard worked together at the British office of an LA-based artist management company called The Firm.

Olly would come to question the endless comparisons with Robbie Williams. It may have been helpful for his name to be mentioned in the same breath as the ex-Take That superstar but it would be important to develop his own style – and fast. 'He might be a hero of mine,' said Olly, 'but I don't want to be his dummy.'

Nevertheless, the two had shared some intimate conversations. When the pair first met, Robbie's first words 'Nice to meet you, Olly' amazed him. 'I thought, "Oh my God, you know my name."' The two chatted back at Robbie's trailer. 'We sat down with no one else there,' Olly would recall in August 2010. 'He was saying what he'd gone through in the past five years, how he's been off drink, how he was feeling such a better person and how much his now-wife Ayda means to him.'

The two bonded and Robbie encouraged Olly to

contact him by email for help and advice. 'It felt like he was taking me under his wing. I sent him congratulations on his wedding and he emailed back saying, "Do you know what, Olly, I'm so happy, I've had a fantastic day."' And it was Robbie who urged Olly to be involved in his career at a creative level and become a songwriter. 'Robbie really pushed songwriting on to me. He said, "When you get signed, make sure you write and make sure you get involved with it." That is where the money is for artists.'

Like the emotive theme song to the film *Love Story*, 'Please Don't Let Me Go' starts with the rhetorical question, 'Where do I begin?' It's an appropriate start for a novice lyricist. Not only was 'Please Don't Let Me Go' Olly Murs's recording debut, it marked his beginning as a songwriter. 'That was one of the things I wanted to get involved in most. I'd never done any writing before but, since the *X Factor* tour finished, I've been going into writing sessions with lots of ideas.'

The ITV2 documentary *Olly Murs Revealed* (which would be screened in the autumn of 2010) followed some of his early attempts at songwriting. He was to have a rude awakening about the rigours of the art, about helping to create something that had a memorable tune, a chorus that everyone could join in with and words that the audience could relate to in some way. 'The frustrating thing about songwriting is actually having something to talk about – an actual scenario,' he said. But one bit of advice would help in his first tentative steps: not being afraid to brainstorm. In order to create anything, you have to be unafraid of taking a risk, try out new lyrics and come up with new ideas. 'One thing I learned is nothing I say is wrong,' he said, referring to the lyric-writing process. 'Even if it just sounds like the most ridiculous lyric, say it.'

Olly knew that helping to write his own material might help him be viewed as an independent spirit in music. There was nothing worse than being branded a 'puppet' in pop, someone who was being controlled by writers and producers behind the scenes. 'There's no one behind me pulling strings,' he said. 'I know I'm never going to be seen as a credible artist. Then again, look at Will Young. One of the best male singers that this country has had in the past 10 years. Now you don't think of *Pop Idol* when you think of him.'

For 'Please Don't Let Me Go', written around April 2010, Olly collaborated with Claude Kelly and Steve Robson. Both had quite a pedigree as pop songwriters. Kelly had written top-selling hits for Miley Cyrus, Kelly Clarkson and Leona Lewis. Robson's credits included songs for James Morrison and Take That. 'When I'm writing and recording, I'm always thinking about the audience and if I think they'll like it,' said Olly.

The song is cannily titled. A singer best known for interpreting cover versions on a reality-TV show (albeit extremely well) was reinventing himself as a serious artist with self-penned material. Was 'Please Don't Let Me Go' a subconscious plea to the music-buying public not to reject or forget him? No one knew if this, his debut solo single, would be a success or not.

In late June, two months before its official release as a single, 'Please Don't Let Me Go' was given a press launch, the start of a period of feverish promotion. The *Sun*'s gossip columnist Gordon Smart talked up the song's charms no end and vowed that, thanks to a loyal fan base, here was a pop star who would be around for some time to come. Hearing echoes of songs by Lily Allen, Paolo Nutini and even some UB40, he celebrated it early as a 'summery pop track'. Plus there were also throwbacks to the 1980s ska-pop of Madness and The Specials, who in their heyday had themselves been reviving ska and reggae traditions of the 1960s.

Olly described the song as 'one you could play in the car with the windows down when the weather's good'. He even confided later that there was another more unpredictable reference point in 'Please Don't Let Me Go' – TV commercials for a certain tropical fruit drink. 'When you hear the Lilt ads in winter, you want to go away [on holiday]. Reggae is the summer sound. I wanted that warm feel on the album.'

The sessions for Olly's album were progressing well. As co-writer, he was following one of the maxims of creativity: write about what you know. 'The songs are about real life – relationships, mates and various situations you find yourself in.' When it came to suitable subject matter as source material for song ideas, Olly looked back to former squeezes from his younger days. 'I've never been in therapy but it's similar because I was going over old relationships where I might have been cheated on and working it through.'

A stockpile of songs was building up. There were reportedly as many as 40 compositions. For the final running order of the album, 12 would be selected, 10 of them co-written by Olly. Four other songs were reserved as bonus material for the single releases. He would come to describe the album as a 'fruit salad' with musical inspiration coming from all directions. As on 'Please Don't Let Me Go', reggae and ska influences were high in the mix, notably the Bob Marley and Specials classics he associated with the summer months. But he cited the work of Jason Mraz, the pop trio Scouting for Girls and, naturally, Robbie Williams as other big influences. 'It's quite like the single, with that reggae feel,' he promised, 'but it's also got some ballads, pop tunes, a lot of uptempo tracks and a lot of me in it.'

Olly, his management and his record company were aware that if you just recorded one type of song in one genre, you would attract a limited audience. It was better to genre-hop, as it would broaden Olly's appeal and make him a more versatile artist to boot. The same way of thinking had been used for choosing his repertoire on *The X Factor* in the previous autumn. If you could tackle big band, ballads, rock, soul and pure pop, and tackle them all with professionalism and style, you were doing well.

Olly's first album was put together over the summer of 2010, for eventual release at the end of November. He would be working with a wide range of other writers and producers, including many creative and experienced people behind some of the biggest hits in pop. 'I'm really happy with the songs,' he said. 'I worked with some amazing writers.' Sometimes, ignorance of his collaborators' success could calm Olly's nerves. Recording at London's Sarm Studios, he had no idea of the status of its owner, the super-producer and writer Trevor Horn. 'And he's sold two-hundred million records! I didn't know him before I met him, I would have been too nervous.'

Horn had quite a history. His best work was both supremely polished and cutting edge. Since his beginnings as a session bass guitarist, he had briefly been a pop star himself when his group Buggles topped the charts all over the world with the naggingly catchy 'Video Killed the Radio Star' in 1979. The song's video even became the first to be shown when the 24-hour music TV channel MTV launched in the USA in 1981. Over the next 30 years, Horn would be record producer to countless hit acts, including Spandau Ballet, ABC, Pet Shop Boys, Rod Stewart, Leann Rimes, Seal, Paul McCartney, Cher and Robbie Williams. At the time Olly was born (1984), Horn had just launched his own record label, ZTT, with one of the most talked-about singles of the time, the controversial number-one hit by Frankie Goes to Hollywood, 'Relax'.

With that wealth, breadth and depth of experience, Horn was on hand to offer plenty of useful advice to a singer in a recording studio. 'It's a very vulnerable thing to walk into a studio and sing into a microphone,' he said. 'You can sound great, then four lines later, you can sound like a complete amateur.' As he worked with Olly on the song which would close his debut album, 'A Million More Years', he reminded him to 'try not to lose any part of the note' he was singing.

'A Million More Years' was co-written by Lol Creme, one of the members of the innovative 1970s pop group 10cc. Just because you weren't a pop star anymore it didn't mean you couldn't be creative, and the list of songwriting credits on Olly's album showed he had joined forces with some major pop names. Chris Difford, who co-wrote the ballad 'Ask Me to Stay', had co-written numerous high-quality and often bittersweet songs for the group Squeeze from the mid-1970s. Their many hits included 'Cool for Cats', 'Up the Junction' and the country-and-western pastiche 'Labelled with Love'.

In the charts more recently had been Preston of the Ordinary Boys, who had helped Olly write 'Don't Say Goodbye'. Future single 'Heart on My Sleeve', one of only two album tracks not to be penned by Olly, had been co-written by James Morrison and had first been recorded by the 2009 winner of *American Idol*, Michael Johns. 'Love Shine Down', with its soul-gospel feel, was partly composed by one Ed Sheeran, before he made a commercial breakthrough in his own right.

If you peruse the names of the songwriters on many contemporary pop albums, they may not seem immediately familiar. But even if you don't know their names, the chances are you will almost certainly know some of the songs they've written. Olly's album was no exception. Between them, the writers had worked on material for Kelly Clarkson, Craig David, Paloma Faith, The Lighthouse Family, Britney Spears, Tina Turner, Westlife and Will Young.

Writing a successful song can be far more lucrative than singing it. Olly Murs had heeded Robbie Williams' advice that he should become a songwriter and he was about to find out how his first compositions would fare with the public.

CHAPTER THIRTEEN

LETTING GO

Early July 2010 would find Olly Murs at Manchester United's home ground of Old Trafford. He was warming up the crowd for the club's annual First Team Open Training Session. But he longed to be on the pitch for the kick-off. 'I've played football ever since I was a little boy; it's always something I wanted to be. I'd actually give up my career now if I could get back and play football, I loved it so much.'

Luckily for him and his record company, who had spent a million pounds on making his album, Olly was not signed up to play for Manchester United. Instead, he busied himself with promoting 'Please Don't Let Me Go'. Even though it would not be on sale until 29 August, it was a favourite with radio stations by mid-July. As he began work on making a video for the song, his label Syco Music announced plans to make a fly-on-the-wall documentary about him for ITV2. The hour-long film would chart his progress over the summer of 2010 and feature Olly talking about his life and career to date. Olly suggested that the film could be called *Life on Murs* 'but we're still not sure'.

Eventually titled *Olly Murs Revealed*, the film was broadcast by ITV2 in November 2010 to coincide with the release of his debut album. The crew had followed him around all summer, filming him in the recording studio, at charity events and promoting his first single release. Along the way, it visited the Murs family home in Witham and tagged along when Olly attended an appointment with a Harley Street doctor who specialised in the larynx, or the 'voicebox'. He explained to Olly how any singer needs to take great care of this most precious physical feature.

In August 2010, *The X Factor* returned to ITV1 for its seventh series. Regular panellist Louis Walsh reiterated that winning the show wasn't everything. 'It's a platform for all kinds of talent – if you've got talent. They're all working it from last year. You don't have to win the show to be successful.'

Although both Olly and Joe McElderry were lined up to guest on the show for the new autumn series, one journalist, Michael Hogan, writing in the *Daily Telegraph*, couldn't help pointing out that 'last year's main success so far has been Jedward – who Cowell disowned as a novelty act'. It was noted that in the '*X Factor* World', the power ballad was still king – at a time when the singles charts were crammed with rap, R&B and dance records.

Was the show losing its touch? A rival series for Sky1 over the 2010 summer called *Must Be the Music*, hosted by Radio 1's Fearne Cotton, tried to place musical brilliance at the centre of the format. With a panel consisting of jazz prodigy Jamie Cullum, lead singer of Texas Sharleen Spiteri and rapper Dizzee Rascal, it invited musicians as well as singers to participate and permitted them to perform their own compositions rather than sing covers.

While *Must Be the Music* crossed its fingers for innovation, *X Factor* 2010's initial audition acts looked in danger of retreading the same ground. Those watching one hopeful in a trendy cap and waistcoat could have been forgiven for thinking Olly Murs already had a tribute act. The more promising Matt Cardle, a singing painter and decorator from Essex, had been offered some tips by the 2009 runner-up. 'He's from down the road,' said Matt of Olly, 'so I got his number from a friend. He had some good words to say to me.' But Matt did admit that he had been pressurised to change his sartorial look, having been urged to ditch the green cap and checked shirts. When competing in *The X Factor*, it was important to be distinctive.

The other major *X Factor*-related headline of the new season was the claim that pitch correction (sometimes known as 'autotune') had been used to enhance the performances of some contestants in early editions of the new series covering the auditions. Cowell soon vowed that the enhancements would not be used again, especially not when people were ringing in to vote and being charged for the privilege.

Olly hotly denied that he had ever mimed on the show but understood why some might want to do so. 'We all get colds, we all get throat infections. If I went up there with a throat infection and couldn't sing, I think I would get even worse feedback from it. So, if the option is there to mime if you can't physically sing, you should.' In other words, the show should go on even if you can't produce the sound. What matters is that the star is present.

So with a new *X Factor* series starting, now was the time for the stars of the previous run to make their mark and remind the public about them, before the new finds of the show had a chance to replace them as national talking points. The release of Olly's 'Please Don't Let Me Go' would coincide with the programme's return. It would appear as the show presented a fresh batch of hopefuls. Just one year before, one of those hopefuls had been Olly.

Despite the plea of its title, there seemed little danger that Olly's fan base would 'let him go'. Quite the reverse, in fact – he seemed more popular than ever, although it was a mystery how some of his fan mail reached him. 'I get all of these letters and cards but the fans just write to "Olly Murs, Essex". I'm not sure how the mail gets to me. It's staggering.' The packages written to this vague address could contain anything from badges to posters, from pants to – yes – trilby hats. As Olly still lived at home with parents Pete and Vicky-Lynn, storage space for all these gifts was beginning to be an issue. 'I've just had an argument with my mum about it,' he said. 'We're going to have to get another room added to the house because they keep sending so much.'

Olly was also familiarising himself with the solo photo shoot, posing for still pictures that would be splashed over magazines and newspapers and for posters which would adorn the walls of all his fans. Happy to participate in a shoot, he wasn't quite so keen to analyse the pictures afterwards. 'I don't like to look at the photos. I always say to the guys, "You're the experts – if you think they look good, they look good."' His stylists and dressers were careful not to go over the top with how they presented him but to make him look as natural and as comfortable as possible. He was at home wearing skinny jeans, and even the signature trilby hat was a touch which had only emerged during *The X Factor.*

Olly's personality – genial, amiable, slightly cheeky – made him a natural for TV bookings: *Alan Carr: Chatty Man*, *Celebrity Juice*, breakfast TV, *This Morning*. In the days of *Top of the Pops* and Saturday morning shows like *Going Live!*, *Live and Kicking* and *CD:UK*, pop coverage had been mainly for the young. Now it was for the young *and* young at heart. Pop stars would often plug their wares on shows aimed at all ages. Olly and his team knew that it wasn't just teenagers who liked him but older listeners as well.

As the days ticked by until the release of 'Please Don't Let Me Go', Olly reflected that 2010 had been busy but low-key for him. Though he had performed in front of many live audiences during the year, cameras had been generally absent. His sets had been dominated by covers from his time on *The X Factor*. From here on, his repertoire would mix standards like 'Don't Stop Me Now' and 'Superstition' with his new, original and self-penned material. 'It's been an amazing, brilliant year,' he gushed in mid-August but added, 'It's just the start of it now.' And he was crossing his fingers that he was about to top the charts in his own right: 'Every artist wants a number one so we're aiming for that. The feedback has been fantastic. I'm just happy, and hopeful we get what we want.'

Despite Olly's sudden success and promising prospects as a recording artist, the Murs family were experiencing a mixed year in 2010. Although his elder sister Fay was about to get married that October, their parents were not having the easiest of times. Not only were doctors still trying to get to the root of Vicky-Lynn's long-term ME-related illness, which had forced her to give up her job in recruitment, but in May, Pete, who was a toolmaker, had suffered an accident at work and broken his leg, meaning that, for the time being, he could not work either. 'The stress mounts up,' Olly admitted. 'It is very difficult and I'm sure they go through a lot. But I think this whole experience has really given them a lift.'

But one awkward line of questioning persisted in interviews. Olly was still being asked about missing his twin brother Ben's wedding the previous December. He remained unrepentant about the path he had taken. 'Looking back, it was the best decision I ever made. If I had gone to the wedding and not got through to the final, I would've always been thinking, "If only I'd stayed for those extra few hours, I might have." You're not always guaranteed a record deal.'

Olly had to admit that all was not well between him and his twin. 'We haven't spoken for a while now,' he said. He hoped that the frosty relations between them could be thawed at sister Fay's wedding in the autumn. But he reckoned without a devastating interview Ben would soon give.

On Sunday, 22 August 2010, the now-defunct Sunday newspaper the *News of the World* published a tell-all interview with Ben. Olly's suggestion that they weren't talking and had fallen out was confirmed. 'I watch my brother on TV now,' said Ben, 'and it's like I don't even know who he is.'

Ben, who worked as a mechanical design engineer, went on to talk about how he felt betrayed, not just towards his brother but towards his whole family. He was upset that they had seemed more entranced by Olly's television appearances than by his wedding. He felt let down that Olly had not congratulated the pair of them live on *The X Factor*. He even claimed that Olly had not told him firsthand that he would not be at the wedding, nor able to fulfil his duties as best man.

'I understand why Olly wasn't at the wedding,' said Ben, who had announced his engagement to Amy in April 2008. 'It clashed with the *X Factor* semi-final and singing has been his dream for years. But what hurt was that he never even told me himself he wasn't going to be able to be my best man.'

Olly's initial response to the *News of the World* splash was one of anger. On the social-networking site Twitter, he wrote, 'Can't believe my own blood, my own family has sold a story on me. It's disgusting. Especially when I wish he told the truth.' He soon removed the message. His official response, quoted in the press two days later, was a little more diplomatic: 'My whole family is upset by this situation which has been apparent for some time and has little to do with me or *The X Factor*. I hope that this private family matter will be resolved soon as I do love Ben and only want the best for him.'

Olly would be regularly asked by reporters and interviewers about the uneasy silence between him and Ben. He maintained a sad resignation about the situation, regarded it as the lowest point of his time in the limelight, and hoped that things would ease. Even so, he had no regrets about the decision he had made. 'Even if I had been allowed to go to Ben's wedding, I still think I would have turned it down. Otherwise, I wouldn't have had the three or four hours' rehearsal time I needed. Unfortunately, I was on a TV show where deadlines were very tight. I've learned that if you fail to prepare, prepare to fail.'

Dealing with an unwelcome private matter that becomes public news can be tricky for a celebrity, especially one who has only just begun to taste fame. When a negative story appears in the papers, do you ignore it or respond to it? Andi Peters, formerly a children's-TV presenter, and later a producer and media consultant, gave Olly some much-needed advice on how to react in the circumstances. You couldn't ignore a question about a subject like that if it arose but, stressed Peters, 'You've got to make sure you close the question down as soon as it's asked.' Peters reminded the new star to keep engaging in direct eye contact with the interviewer and to always give an answer as a sentence which had a start, a middle and an end.

The unhappy experience of reading the interview with his brother was a reminder to Olly that part of stardom is learning to accept rocky patches as part of the roller-coaster ride of fame. Several artists he idolised – the likes of Michael Bublé, Stevie Wonder and, of course, Robbie Williams – had had their ups and downs in their lives. 'But they've come through, they are still massive stars and they have managed to keep hold of themselves.'

At lunchtime on Monday, 30 August 2010, the day after it was first made available as a digital download, Olly Murs celebrated the physical release of his debut solo single 'Please Don't Let Me Go' by making a special appearance in Essex. He performed a free acoustic show at the HMV store in Chelmsford, and had a kiss and a hug ready for the few hundred lucky people who showed up.

Olly and his record label crossed their fingers that 'Please Don't Let Me Go' would enter the charts at the highest possible position, ideally at number one. But he was up against popular tracks from the then-current number one Taio Cruz, along with Eminem and Rihanna, plus new singles from Katy Perry and Kanye West. Another act strongly tipped for glory was a new duo called Pepper and Piano, discovered on Sky1's *Must Be the Music*, whose song 'You Took My Heart' (about recovering from drug addiction) had the support of Lily Allen. The duo's debut hit would ultimately peak at number seven.

In the event, Olly would outsell all competition. The nine weeks of relentlessly promoting 'Please Don't Let Me Go', not to mention the graft in creating the single itself, had paid off. On Sunday, 5 September, it was announced that his solo debut had edged ahead of Katy Perry's 'Teenage Dream' and topped the UK charts, dethroning Taio Cruz's 'Dynamite'. Even the bonus track on 'Please Don't Let Me Go', 'This One's for the Girls', charted (on digital downloads only), albeit much more modestly at number 69.

'I'm absolutely over the moon,' Olly gasped about becoming top of the pops. 'Especially as I was up against such stiff competition. Thank you so much to all my fans.' He was particularly glad that his single had beaten Katy Perry to number one. 'When we first got told she was releasing that week, it kind of kicked us all in the nuts, if I'm honest,' he later admitted.

Though the single had received plenty of exposure on commercial radio stations around Britain, it was more coolly received by the producers at BBC Radio 1. The song had not been included on the station's official playlist, a decision which breakfast show host Chris Moyles vehemently disagreed with. 'Whoever said no was wrong,' said Moyles. 'If you're saying, "No, I don't want to hear it," and it becomes the most popular record of the week, you're wrong.' For his part, Olly conceded that maybe he wasn't going to be the most cutting-edge of artists. 'I know that I'm never going to be classified as a credible artist, I'm never going to be in the *NME*. But I'm proud to be part of the *X Factor* family.'

When 'Please Don't Let Me Go' entered the UK singles charts at number one, Olly was obliged to honour a promise he had made to the readers of *Heat* magazine. 'I said if I get to number one, I'll do a naked photo shoot. Every gig I do [my fans] try to get me to take my clothes off, so it's a promise to them.' Cries of 'Get your top off' had become common to members of Olly's fan base but he insisted that the naked shoot would be a one-off. 'I'll probably be really nervous. I hate getting my body out but I'll do it for my fans. I won't let them down.'

He accepted that not everyone would want to see the nude shot but he wanted to please the fans who had bought his single. He set about preparing for the shoot, which was to take place on Thursday, 9 September, and announced that he might tone up in the gym with the boys from JLS. 'I'll have a wax before I do it,' he promised. 'I'm a bit hairy on the top half so I might have to trim that down. I'll also need to have a little tidy-up down below. It will make it look bigger.'

Would that be strictly necessary? Something would

have to cover his modesty when naked. Maybe a piece of fruit but which one? 'Without doubt, a pineapple,' Olly cheekily insisted. 'Glad he didn't say "Satsuma",' quipped the *Sun*'s resident gossipmonger, Gordon Smart. In the event, the prop that Olly opted to use was some headgear. For once, it wasn't a trilby but a bowler hat.

Female staffers at *Heat* were particularly keen to watch this photo shoot for some unknown reason. Only one actually needed to be present but a further three found that they could manage to clear their schedules.

As he started packing for a well-earned break – a stag weekend in Ibiza with 22 of his friends – Olly was relieved that he had established himself in a big way as a solo artist, nearly nine months after failing to win *The X Factor*. There had been immense pressure on 'Please Don't Let Me Go' to make as big an impression as possible (both in terms of sales and airplay), and there hadn't been time for him to build up a following via demos and low-key gigs. 'If I'd released my first single and it went in the charts at number twenty, I'd have been dropped [by the record label], no question. But had that happened, I'd still have no regrets about any of it. None at all.'

Olly's rise to stardom.

Above: Attending a secret gig for *The X Factor* semi-finalists alongside fellow contestants Danyl Johnson, Stacey Solomon and Joe McElderry in 2009.

Below left: Olly with the eventual *X Factor* winner Joe.

Below right: A year after becoming runner-up on *The X Factor*, Olly made his first performance as a solo artist at G-A-Y in London.

Taking it all in his stride: performing for his fans at T4 on the Beach in Weston-super-Mare.

Super talented
Olly was asked to
co-present ITV2's
The Xtra Factor
with Caroline
Flack in 2011.

Olly always has time for his fans.

Above left: Ready to sign copies of his CD.

Above right and *below*: Meeting and greeting some lucky fans!

The BRIT Awards, 2012. Even though Olly is the cheeky chappie boy-next-door, known for his trendy style, he still likes to look the part for award shows.

Above: Performing for a TV crew.

Below: Backstage at the Royal Albert Hall in 2011 with *X Factor* judge, Take That star Gary Barlow, plus his protégé Marcus Collins.

Olly has achieved so much since taking part in *The X Factor*.

Above: Lapping up the applause at Birmingham's LG Arena in 2012.

Below: Performing his hit song 'Heart Skips a Beat' and demonstrating why he's a true British icon.

Doing what he does best: performing for his fans!